"Moms make a difference with their sons. Rhonda leads us on an important journey with humor, authenticity, and transparency, learning from the moms found in the pages of Scripture. I found it so refreshing to look at them with the new lens Rhonda offers. This book is for every mom—whether just starting out or in the midst of raising a son. Perhaps most important for many moms is the thoughtful way Rhonda brings encouragement when a son wanders far from God. While the whole book is a blessing, I believe that Part Three, "Even if...," will wash over the hearts and souls of many and replace the despair of a prodigal with peace and hope."

Ed Gossien, chief ministry officer at Awana

"Moms, this is a book you need. In a culture filled with confusion about what healthy masculinity looks like, Rhonda Stoppe offers clarity and hope as you raise your sons to be godly young men. The insights and guidance she provides in these pages are so urgently needed today."

Bob Lepine, author, *Build a Stronger Marriage*, pastor,
Redeemer Community Church of Little Rock

"The role of motherhood is the most underrated and yet impactful role in society. Oh, how our world needs strong men to stand up and be counted, to lead their family with wisdom and love, to serve God! *Moms Raising Sons to Be Men* inspires and encourages mums on their journey. Thank you, Rhonda, for your stories and words of wisdom."

Helen Smallbone, author, *Behind the Lights*, and
cofounder of MUMlife Community

"There's no question that our culture has muddied the waters and sown great confusion about manhood. Rhonda Stoppe's clear, wise, and scripturally grounded perspective and advice are sure to empower moms seeking to raise their sons to reflect Christ's character and further His kingdom."

John Fuller, vice president, Focus on the Family

"How can a mother nurture her son in our floundering world where men of integrity are in short supply? What hope is there for single moms and broken homes in our alien society? With expertise and compassion, Rhonda Stoppe guides readers through biblical truths and commonsense solutions to assure it can be done. Meaningful manhood, she writes, begins with a discerning, dedicated mother. Here is a book every boy's mom needs."

Jeanne Hendricks, author, wife of the late Howard G. Hendricks
(Professor, Dallas Theological Seminary)

"What a powerful perspective! Rhonda has a solid understanding of what the Bible says about mothers and sons, and she uses real-life examples and a tell-it-like-it-is style of wisdom that is needed for this day and age. This book offers great advice for mothers to raise their sons to be men who can affect generations to come."

Matthew West, GRAMMY-nominated recording artist

"This book parallels parenting itself—humorous, eye-opening, challenging, and rewarding all at the same time. It's a must for any mother who understands the incredible influence she has on her son(s), and who desires to be a faithful steward of this privileged task—and have some fun along the way. The insights Rhonda shares by using the blueprint of God's Word are a gift that will inspire a new generation of world-changing mothers."

Phil Joel, musician, songwriter, and founder of deliberatePeople ministries

"Rhonda is real! She shares honestly and vulnerably her mistakes as well as her victories when it comes to raising boys into strong, God-following men. Through her sound biblical advice, her godly insights, and her practical wisdom, you will be encouraged, enlightened, and empowered to become the mom you've always wanted to be—and to guide your son into becoming the man God intended."

Cindi McMenamin, national speaker and author of *When Women Walk Alone*

"I have interacted with many young men over the years who have been either positively or negatively impacted by their mother's example. This book will prove to be a challenging and practical exhortation for moms to fulfill their calling to be women of the Word who influence their sons to be men of God."

Jake Ebner, The Master's College, Santa Clarita, CA

MOMS
RAISING SONS
to Be MEN

RHONDA STOPPE

HARVEST HOUSE PUBLISHERS
EUGENE, OREGON

Published in association with the literary agency of The Steve Laube Agency, LLC, 24 W. Camelback Rd. A-635, Phoenix, Arizona 85013.

For bulk, special sales, or ministry purchases, please call 1-800-547-8979.
Email: Customerservice@hhpbooks.com

Cover design by Studio Gearbox

Interior design by Chad Dougherty

Interior photos by Jessica Gardner Photography

Podcast photo by Family Life Photography, Indirah Michmerhuizen

Cover photo © Cat_arch_angel / Shutterstock

M This logo is a federally registered trademark of the Hawkins Children's LLC. Harvest House Publishers, Inc., is the exclusive licensee of this trademark.

Moms Raising Sons to Be Men

To my sons,
Tony Hebert and Brandon Stoppe,
who continually encouraged me as I wrote this book,
and to my precious sons-in-law,
Jacob Ebner and Estevan Atkinson
I am richly blessed to have watched each of you
become godly men in this generation.
The world is a better place because of your faith
and resolve to follow Christ.

To my daughters
Meredith, Kayla, Kylene, and Jessy
I'm amazed by your wisdom and grace.
You truly are the godly architects of the next generation!

And finally, to our fifteen grandchildren
(and any others God may bless us with)
May God capture each of your hearts to live in
wholehearted devotion to Jesus.
I pray that your love for God and for others will turn
the world upside down for Christ
and shine brightly the hope of the gospel
in your generation.

Soli Deo gloria

CONTENTS

INTRODUCTION

Guiding your son toward manhood is the most exciting, terrifying, exhilarating, exhausting, and rewarding calling from the Lord. I've raised two sons and two daughters, and we now have 15 grandchildren—so I've been in your shoes, friend.

I remember how intimidated I was when I pondered all that could go wrong if I didn't raise my son well. Are you a new mom with hopes and dreams for your son's future? Maybe you're looking around at young men who have rebelled against their Christian upbringing, or perhaps you are a mom who is now picking up the pieces of a life upended by your son's rebellion.

In more than 30 years of ministry, alongside my pastor-husband, we have had the privilege of watching God work in and through parents who weren't super confident about their roles. But God, who promises to be strength in your weakness, is glorified when you seek His wisdom and guidance for the ministry to which He calls you.

In this book you will find inspiration and wisdom from mothers in history, moms of the Bible, and present-day mothers whose sons influenced their generation for Christ. Do you realize that the first teachers of powerful, godly, world changers were their mothers?

I can't wait to share some of their stories with you! And just as God called those mothers in their generation, He is now calling *you* to this incredible ministry of guiding your son toward knowing, loving, and serving Christ in his generation.

Don't be intimidated. You are not alone, Momma. A throng of mothers has charted this path ahead of you—ready to cheer you on and share with you what we have learned.

Wherever you find yourself in your parenting journey, please walk with me through the pages of this book. I know life is busy and reading a book can seem like just one more thing on your to-do list. I get it. But if all you can manage is to read five or ten minutes a day, you will progress through these life-changing principles to help guide you in your motherhood journey. Together we will unlock important secrets to guide your son toward a life without regrets.

I'll be cheering you on every step of the way. I would love to receive a note from you. And when you email, let me know you're reading my book, and I'll send you a free link to watch my video: *How to Raise a Son to Be a Good Man.*

You can email: rhonda@noregretswoman.com

Brandon, Rhonda, and Tony

PART ONE

LIFE LESSONS FROM MOMS OF THE BIBLE

CHAPTER 1

YOU ARE NOT ALONE

On Mission with God

Luke was 13 years old and had become quite a good tennis player. One day he was playing in a tennis tournament. As he watched the match preceding his, he became convinced that he would have no problem winning against his next opponent. However, during the match, he became inconsistent and was not doing his best.

Luke got very angry with himself. He threw down his racket and chastised himself for making a mistake. Amid his temper tantrum, he looked up into the audience in time to see his mother, Helen, get up and leave the stands. Luke lost his match that day, and Helen never returned to the event.

Later, Helen met Luke at the car. Driving home, she explained to him why she had walked out: "I will not witness my son showing such disrespect. Your actions today did not display a man who was emulating Christ."

Luke Smallbone is one of seven children raised by Helen and her husband, David. Helen's oldest daughter is Rebecca St. James, a well-known Christian singer. Luke and his brother, Joel, also make their living as Christian musicians with their popular band for KING & COUNTRY. Luke says all his siblings have grown up to serve the Lord, and he attributes that to how his parents raised them to surrender their talents to God. "Keep your hands open. Be willing to take a risk," Helen often told her children.

Luke says, "My mother always made it a point to have the hard conversations with me and my siblings. My parents taught me to think. They were good at answering my questions. By taking the time to walk my thought process through the answers, they helped me learn to weigh out the possible consequences of my actions. My mother always cherished us, with the perfect balance of love and a discipline that said, 'I am for you. I believe in you. I see who the real Luke is. I know God has something in store for you.'"

When I asked Luke to describe his mother's influence upon the man he has become, he said, "My mother is strong, compassionate, and caring, all mixed into one. She raised me with incredible care and honesty. I probably owe all that I am and have achieved to my mom because when a man is loved by his mother, he can end up doing great things…I am grateful to have a mother who selflessly loved me."

In her memoir, *Behind the Lights*, Helen Smallbone says, "Deep down, I believe every mum is an unsung hero." [1] Helen's life and legacy certainly attests to the influence a mom can have upon her children and the culture in which they live. How did Helen raise all seven of her children—five boys and two girls—to love and serve the Lord? What can we learn from her? And to what can we attribute her success?

Ken Sande, author of *The Peacemaker*, says, "The world defines success in terms of what a person possesses, controls, or accomplishes. God defines success in terms of faithful obedience to His will. The world asks, 'What results have you achieved?' God asks, 'Were you faithful to my ways?'…He asks for only one thing—obedience to His revealed will." [2]

Your success as a mother does not depend upon what your son

chooses to do with his life. Rather, according to Scripture, success lies in *your* obedience to God—in what *you* choose to do with your life.

If you get nothing else out of this book, get this: God has called you to the ministry of motherhood. And with that calling He has provided the Holy Spirit to lead you and guide you in your journey. By being committed to know God through His Word, you will grow to love Him more each day, and when you love God properly, you will love your son correctly. The Lord has provided tools for you to do well in your calling. By daily communing with Him through the Bible, prayer, worship, and fellowship with the church, you will be fully equipped for this incredible privilege of bringing up your son, because God will work through you to raise your son for His glory.

To be the mother of a son is not for the faint of heart. I remember when my son Brandon was born. Looking into his little face, the feelings within me were somehow different from four years earlier when I had given birth to my daughter. I felt so inadequate as I weighed the responsibility of molding this baby into a man. Up to this point, raising a girl had not been a difficult challenge. It was clear that she was like me, with all the love for being a girl that she could express. She loved shoes and colorful bows for her hair. She was extremely social and adored her friends. And her daddy? Oh, she loved her daddy. Yes, relating to her had been no problem at all.

Yet now in my arms I was holding a helpless baby boy who would grow into a man. In her book *Strong Mothers, Strong Sons*, Dr. Meg Meeker explains: "The mother-son dyad is complicated by the opposition of gender. Neither mother nor son can fully understand what it is like to be the other half of the equation."[3] My biggest concern was that I would mess up as a mom, and my failure would lead to his rebellion. Maybe you have had similar concerns.

When you gave birth to your son, did you find yourself imagining what kind of man he might become? When it came to my son, I did not want to raise a momma's boy, yet I wanted to be his protector. I did not want him to be rough and reckless, but I did want him to be strong. I wanted him to become a wonderful, godly man like his father. After I took the little guy home and began to raise him, I found my parenting overshadowed by a fear of doing it wrong. I gradually developed a sort of reactionary mode—he acted, and I reacted. Rather than following a clear path toward shaping his life, the fear of what I did *not* want my son to be became my standard. I was merely putting out fires rather than kindling the flames of my son's character.

My husband and I had always wanted our home to be a place of peace, yet I found it becoming a chaotic environment ruled by *my* emotions. Because I did not want to disappoint my husband, I did not let him know how much I was struggling. The day my daughter said to me, "I know you can't wait until we are grown up so you can do whatever you want," was the day I knew I needed to get some help. It broke my heart that I had given her that notion. I loved being a mother; it was what I *wanted* to do. Yet in my harried frustration, that was not at all the impression I had given my sweet little girl.

Feeling even more inadequate and alone, I began to read books about parenting, from which I compiled a sort of how-to list. I soon discovered that the list did not have the power to change me. It became a burdensome reminder of the standard I was unable to meet. I lacked fortitude for this new adventure. I knew I needed to *become* a kind, courageous, and confident mother if I was ever going to raise kind, courageous, confident children. I desired to be a godly mother who raised godly children. But where would I find the direction I so desperately longed for?

I Need Help, Lord!

Reading books had given me some basic ground rules for this new playing field, but I also wanted to learn from the women around me. My mother-in-law, who had raised two wonderful sons, had been diagnosed with Alzheimer's disease and was no longer the vibrant help she had been when my daughter was born. The young mothers I knew seemed no more prepared for raising a son than I was. I felt alone and desperate for answers, and I had no idea how to ask God for what I needed. I've since learned that one of God's favorite prayers is that of a simple cry for help flowing from a humble and desperate heart. I was both humbled and desperate as I uttered the plea, "I need help, Lord."

God graciously answered my prayer by bringing several older, godly women into my life. These women were not scholars or trained in child development. But as mothers of sons, they had traveled down this path ahead of me. They had insights and understanding into what I was experiencing. Their lives had not been perfect or free from trials. They were genuine, precious, and vulnerable as they taught me what God had taught them. When I shared my struggles, I did not feel judged; rather, I felt loved.

Titus 2:4 instructs older women to admonish younger women how to love their husbands and their children, and this group of women wholeheartedly obeyed that command. Of all the friendships I have had, the relationships that developed with these women have by far been the most pivotal in my life. They taught me not only how to parent, but also how to *become* the mother God wanted me to become. In writing this book, my heart's desire is to be an older woman God can use to pour courage and confidence into you, just as those women did for me.

The Mission of Motherhood

One life-changing insight I received from these wonderful women was that I had been called by God to the mission of motherhood. And so have you. God has called you to join Him in the work He plans to do in your children. To become the instrument God will use to train your son somehow sheds glorious light on the unique ministry of motherhood, doesn't it? The Bible instructs God's servants to "take heed to the ministry which you have received in the Lord, that you may fulfill it" (Colossians 4:17). There is no pass. No get-out-of-jail-free card. Your ministry came in the form of your son. How will you prepare yourself for that ministry? God never intended mothers to go it alone. Through His Word and godly mentors, He wants to equip you to train your children to love and trust Him.

As you parent your children, if your focus is on every turn of events, you will certainly be overwhelmed and afraid. Fear and confusion will rob you of courage. By contrast, focusing on God and resting in His character will bring peace. Rather than subjecting your family to the gyrations of your emotional reactions, you can develop the habit of responding with an unwavering confidence in who God is. Knowing God intimately is a vital attribute of being a godly mother. How does one develop that kind of confidence in God? I looked to these older women for answers, and they directed me to the Bible.

When I spent time with these women, I observed their peaceful responses to the chaos of life. They didn't trigger when life got hard. Rather, they displayed a resolve to seek after the Lord in every situation. In my estimation, the greatest measure of their parenting success was their sons' genuine love for them *and* for the Lord.

The Crossroad

I found myself at a crossroad when the women encouraged me to attend their ladies' Bible study. Honestly, my motivation was, *Free babysitting and two hours with grown-ups? I'm in!*

During the first session I was given a homework book. I thought, *Homework? No problem.* I had gone to Christian schools; I could fill in the blanks without even having to look up the verses. I know, my response was arrogant. *I* was arrogant! (God would reveal that to me later, but that is a topic for another chapter.)

When I got home and opened the book, I was blown away by

how much work I had to do. This was not the typical fill-in-the-blank book. This was a Precept Ministries International Bible study that assigned five hours of homework each week. Evidently my new friends were under the impression that I had time on my hands. There was no way I could do that much homework! I concluded that these women had their children so long ago they had forgotten how much was needed to care for a baby. When I called my friend Gayle to explain I couldn't possibly keep up with the class, she kindly encouraged me to hang in there for just one semester. She offered to help me by babysitting, promising that I would be forever changed by the experience. I reluctantly agreed to her offer; I didn't want her to think I wasn't spiritual.

I kept the study book open on my kitchen table and worked on the assignments a little bit at a time. I studied while nursing and in between changing diapers and folding laundry. Do you know what I found? For the first time in my life, I began to crave the Word of God. I looked forward to my few minutes of open time here and there to learn from Him. I began to be transformed by the renewing of my mind (Romans 12:2). My thinking was different. My parenting was different. Life's experiences were being filtered through God's truth, and that truth was changing who I was.

Even my husband, Steve, noticed the change. Fear was replaced with peace, anxiety with confidence. My propensity toward people-pleasing was overshadowed by a genuine desire to please God. I had given my heart to Christ when I was young, but never before had I experienced this kind of longing to know Him. Up till now I had always viewed reading the Bible as a religious duty. But this was no duty: I was hungry for God and His Word. I was developing an unwavering resolve to seek God.

Do you long to seek after God? Are you hungering after His Word? Are you eager to cultivate a deeper personal relationship with the One who created you, knows your heart better than anyone else, and provides for your every need? Or perhaps as you're reading this you realize you've never taken that step to surrender to Christ as your Savior and Lord. Or maybe you're uncertain as to whether you are a Christian. If you would like to know more about giving your heart to Christ and having an intimate relationship with Him, please see "How to Have a Relationship with Jesus" on page 225.

Resolve to Seek God

So what does this resolve look like—this hungering and thirsting after God? I read a passage that spoke what my heart longed to express: "My heart is steadfast, O God, my heart is steadfast" (Psalm 57:7). When I read that, I felt I had to know more about the person who penned that phrase! Those words were written by David amid one of the greatest trials of his young life. What kind of woman had raised a son like this? I wanted to live how he lived, and even more, I wanted to raise my son to be like him.

David, while not without his faults, was devoted to seeking God. In Psalm 89:20, God proclaimed, "I have found My servant David." Note that God said He found David. Elsewhere in Scripture we read that "The eyes of the LORD run to and fro throughout the whole earth, to show Himself strong on behalf of those whose heart is loyal to Him" (2 Chronicles 16:9). Can you picture that? The eyes of God moving all across the earth in search of individuals whose hearts are loyal to Him. Why? So that He can show Himself mighty on their behalf. Isn't that exciting? You don't have to do this mother thing alone. God stands ready to offer you His strength. He is even more concerned about the man your son becomes than you are!

Learning to love God will make your heart loyal to Him. When I say this, I'm not talking about being a religious woman—that is, someone who merely goes through the motions of religious duty and rituals in the hopes that you can somehow earn God's favor. No, I'm talking about genuine change that starts in the heart and draws upon God's power and wisdom. I'm talking about a true inner love and passion for God, not mere external behavior that might look good to others but amounts to nothing more than hollow actions. The loyalty God seeks comes from the heart.

The Holy Spirit can use your loyal heart to draw your son to know and obey God. If your faith isn't authentic, your son will know it, and that will likely turn him away from the things of God. It is only as you truly love God and surrender to His perfect will that you are enabled to live as an example to your son and make God attractive to him.

I Surrender All?

David was willing to do anything God asked of him. God said, "I have found David the son of Jesse, a man after My own heart, who will do all My will" (Acts 13:22). As David was growing up, he expressed his love for God in his psalms of worship. Out of that love grew trust. When David was just a young shepherd boy, God allowed him to experience circumstances that would help to build that trust and give him courage for the trials he would face in the future. Don't be deceived into believing that a good God doesn't send trials to His servants. That misconception will cause you to question God's goodness when trouble comes your way. For example, as a young boy, God gave David strength to fight a lion and a bear, knowing full well it would prepare David to battle a giant (1 Samuel 17:36-37).

Mom, you have no idea what giants lie in your son's future. God knows. And while it is tempting to question God's goodness when He allows trials in the life of your children, learn to trust His ways and stay faithful to Christ. In the 30 years that we have been in ministry, we have witnessed many mothers turn away from God when their child endures an unexpected trial. At some point, if the parent is a true believer, they will repent and return to Christ. But at what cost? Your children are observing how you respond to trials to determine if your faith is genuine. How you respond is what God can use to grow their faith and equip them for their future.

For example, my teenaged daughter, Meredith, observed how I chose to trust the Lord while Brandon endured years of severe seizures. A decade later, Meredith would give birth to her own child with special needs. Because Meredith had watched us resolve to follow God when the trial didn't make sense, she was ready to trust Him in her own season of trouble.

Wisdom from David's Mother

Have you ever asked yourself where David's momma was while he was out there camping with the sheep and wrestling wild animals? Well, she wasn't there fighting his battles for him. If my adolescent son had come home and told his daddy that he just battled a bear, I would have pulled my husband aside and said, "He doesn't work for you anymore!" We can learn a lot from David's mom.

She allowed her boy to become a man while he was still living at home. David was her youngest son, yet she allowed him to leave the safety of home to do the dangerous work of a shepherd. What kind of man might he have been if his mother's fears kept him tied to her apron strings? She seemed to know when to step back and allow him to face challenges without micromanaging his choices.

It can be frightening to loosen your grip on your son as he matures. All too often mothers coddle their sons in an attempt to protect them or make life easier for them, only to hinder their ability to manage themselves when they leave the safety of their homes. Making a conscious effort to allow and even orchestrate opportunities for your son to accomplish tasks away from your watchful eye will show him your respect while developing his courage and his ability to make decisions.

She had the courage to leave his safety in the hands of God. In those lonely hours spent on the hillsides, David learned how to be a man. God had used trials to develop his loyal heart. David's mother seemed to have resisted the temptation to rescue him at every turn. The Bible says, "Trust in the LORD with all your heart, and lean not on your own understanding; in all your ways acknowledge Him, and He shall direct your paths" (Proverbs 3:5-6). The Lord wants to be involved in your parenting decisions moment by moment. As you trust and acknowledge Him at each turn, He will make your path straight. If you rely on your own understanding and fight every battle for your son, how will he learn to rely on God's strength?

She respected her husband's wisdom. When David was a teenager, his father, Jesse, sent him to the battlefront with food for his older brothers. You don't hear David's mother protesting, "Not my baby! He is too young to go."

Over the years there have been many times that my husband has given one of our boys a responsibility that I thought was too much for him. My initial instinct was to come to the boy's defense and explain why my husband was making a wrong decision. More often than not, I was the one in the wrong. I had to learn that my husband, who *was* a man, had more discernment with regard to what our sons could and couldn't handle.

David's mother raised a man after God's heart. Do you want to do the same with your son? What kind of mother might you be if you resolved to seek after God more diligently? How would your surrendered life affect your son's character development?

A Courageous Mother

I imagine you would agree that you are bringing your son up in a very difficult time in history. But be encouraged, you're not alone. Mothers down through history have raised their children amid unprecedented difficulties and oppression. Consider the biblical account of another courageous mother.

Moses was another man who was used greatly by God. Who was his mother? Jochebed found herself in a troubled time in Israel's history. Pharaoh sent out a proclamation that every baby boy born to the Hebrew women should be put to death.

When Jochebed and her husband, Amram, gave birth to Moses,

they did their best to hide their lovely son for as long as they could. But after three months, they realized it was only a matter of time before Moses was discovered and killed. Something had to be done, or surely he would end up dying (Exodus 1:15–2:10; Hebrews 11:23).

I can only imagine the ache in Jochebed's heart as she carefully wrapped her precious baby boy in her favorite blanket. As tears streamed down her face, would she have attempted a brave smile into his little face? As if to somehow give him the courage she may desperately have needed for herself?

As Jochebed prepared to place Moses in a basket upon the Nile River, her daughter, who was standing nearby, would likely have questioned the rationale of her mother's plan. "You're putting him in a *basket*, Mother? Will it float? What if water leaks in? What about the snakes and crocodiles?" Surely Jochebed had already asked herself these questions as well. Could this *really* be Jehovah's answer to her prayer to save her son? She must have been confident her idea was from the Lord to even attempt the plan. And yet, would she end up wavering in her conviction as she prepared to send her son afloat on the Nile River?

I am in awe of Jochebed's composure here. Rather than ranting and raving to Amram about their difficult situation, which I am ashamed to say would have been my default mode, she carefully built a little ark for her son. Instead of running to each of her girl-friends for advice, she quietly acted on the plan that God had put in her heart.

We are truly living in troubled times. And while it is tempting to wonder where God is when the world is in such chaos, remember Jochebed's courage to trust God. She simply did the next thing that He put in her heart to do. My advice to you? Do the next thing, Momma. God will work out the details.

How puzzled the people in Jochebed's generation must have been. God had called Israel His chosen people, yet He allowed them to suffer greatly. How is it possible to place your trust in God when your circumstances appear to be wildly out of His control? Do you think you could have sent your baby boy down the Nile River? Imagine watching him float out of your secure hands into the unknown. Where would a mother find the courage to do such a thing?

As Jochebed watched her baby float away, she demonstrated courage that was not found in her ability to preserve the life of her young son. Her decision that day required she follow a plan that had no answers. Yet she sent the baby *away* from her protection and into the care of her God. That kind of courage comes only in the life of one who has developed a genuine trust in Him. Jochebed's confidence in the Lord was evident in her actions.

If Jochebed had tightened her grip on baby Moses and attempted to continue hiding him, she would not have experienced what happened next. Her trusting obedience was rewarded with nothing short of a miracle. When the daughter of Pharaoh drew the little Hebrew baby from the basket floating on the Nile, the Lord moved the princess's heart to compassion. Not only did the Egyptian princess proclaim she would adopt Moses as her son; she sent his very own sister—who happened to be nearby—to find a nursemaid for the baby. And of course, Moses's sister pointed Pharaoh's daughter to Moses's own mother! God blessed Jochebed's obedience by making her Moses's nursemaid.

During the few years Jochebed was permitted to nurse her son, she would have had a profound influence upon him. Surely Jochebed would have told little Moses stories of the faithfulness of the God of Israel. Knowing their time together would not be long, Jochebed would likely have had a sense of urgency to teach Moses to love her God. We mothers would do well to begin developing our children's love for God in their earliest years.

Never underestimate the amount of influence you can have on your son in his first years of life. Intentional togetherness with your infant will play a key role in shaping his brain during the first year of life. Though Jochebed had a very short time to influence Moses, the impression she made was strong enough that it stayed with him even when he grew older and lived in Pharaoh's palace. Her teachings were likely the foundation God used to build Moses's faith. And sure enough, when Moses grew older, he chose to suffer with his people rather than enjoy the pleasures of sin for a season in the palaces of Egypt (Hebrews 11:24-25).

The Bible does not say much about Jochebed and her character qualities. Her name, in Hebrew, means "Jehovah glorified." *Glorified*, as used here, means "to make weighty, to make glorious." Jochebed's actions certainly lived up to her name. In her decision to trust Jehovah, His name was made glorious.

The Influence of a Few Years

The Lord did not bring our oldest boy, Tony, into our lives until he was 15 years old. For years our family has attempted to find a way to illustrate to people, in a clear way, how Tony became our son. One day Tony, now in his forties, called me, excited about a movie he had watched. He said, "I know I am not a big football player like the guy in the movie, but what I saw reminds me so much of our family. And the mom in the movie reminds me of you!" I had seen the very popular movie only days before. I had cried while watching it because it brought back memories of when Tony first came to live with us. He lived in our home for only a short time, but just as the Lord had used Jochebed's few years with Moses to shape him for life, God gave us a brief window of opportunity to give Tony a strong foundation.

Tony had already bonded with Steve even before he moved in with us. Steve was his youth pastor, and right from the beginning they enjoyed a wonderful relationship. When Tony graduated from high school, he gave "Big Steve," as he called him, a card thanking him for becoming his dad. It was a touching note that Steve still keeps with his most treasured possessions. We kind of look at that card as Tony's "official adoption papers."

During Tony's short time with us, he and I had great talks about his new life as a believer, and we talked about girls. We talked about his dream to become a fighter pilot, about God's character, and about girls. We discussed God's plan for marriage…and did I mention we talked about girls?

While Tony and I got along well, he related to me with love and respect, but never as his momma. I wanted to be a mom to him, but I respected that he had a mother whom he loved, and that he didn't necessarily need another.

Upon graduating from high school, Tony was accepted to Texas A&M University. It was difficult for our family to say goodbye to him, but we were excited about the opportunities before him. I determined that my new role in his life would be as a prayer supporter.

Right away Tony, our overachiever, went out for the drill team, a much sought-after and competitive position. The requirements were grueling. All the while, he was taking a full load of classes. By September, Tony had been selected for the team and he was thrilled—thrilled and exhausted.

One day Tony called home. In a weak and shaky voice, he said he had a severe case of pneumonia and would need to take a break from all activities. He told me he was not going to tell his drill commander he was sick for fear of losing his place on the team. Oh my sweet boy, who had worked so hard to achieve his goals! He had been such a man and accomplished great things. Now all I could hear was a little boy who needed a mother.

I asked the Lord for discernment. As I said earlier, we as mothers need to learn when God wants us to step back and allow our young men to battle their trials alone. But somehow I sensed this was different. Tony had worked so hard to land a spot on the team, and now he was terribly sick. I felt that the least I could do was *ask* Tony if I could make a phone call on his behalf. Reluctantly, he agreed.

I called a friend of Tony's who was an alumnus of the school. He promised to make some calls. Soon I heard back from the drill team's commandant, who called to assure me that Tony's place on the team was secure. With that taken care of, we brought our very sick boy home, and I took care of him until he got better. Through that experience, God knit our hearts together, and I became a momma to Tony.

Tony went on to graduate from college and became an F-22 fighter pilot. He is now a lieutenant colonel. While he has achieved many amazing goals, I was never more proud of him than on the day he called to say, "You know, I am living my dream, and I now realize that it is not enough. My Sunday school teacher, a retired fighter pilot, told me that if I am doing all of this but I'm not surrendered to Christ, my life will be wasted."

When asked how being a part of our family influenced him, Tony said, "The family was, and continues to be, my living definition of both what God expects from me, and what He wants for me. I am thankful for this example, and I have no doubt that it was God's plan for our lives to connect."

Only God Knows

Jochebed had no idea she was being used by the Lord to train a child who would one day become the deliverer of Israel. When David's mother sent her young son to the battlefront, how could she have known God had been preparing him to slay a giant? And would she have ever dreamed that her gentle warrior would one day be the king of Israel, as well as a man after God's own heart?

I say all that to bring up this very important point: The first teachers of these godly leaders were not theologians; they were mothers. And you are your son's first teacher about God as well. Generation after generation, the mission of motherhood has been the same. God invites mothers to join Him in molding the character of their sons. Will you partner with God in teaching your son how to love Him? The Word of God is your textbook. Will you determine to prepare yourself for this ministry? The Lord is searching for hearts that are loyal to Him. The same One who called the mothers of Moses and David is calling you. Only God knows the future that awaits your son. What an amazing honor He has given you. *You* are the vessel that the Lord will use to prepare your son for a lifetime of use by Him.

> The first teachers of these godly leaders were not theologians; they were mothers.

THINKING IT THROUGH

Which mother in this chapter do you identify with most? Why?

Have you ever considered motherhood as a ministry? What steps will you start taking now to equip yourself to fulfill this ministry?

LIVING IT OUT

Write out and memorize Psalm 57:7. Will you resolve to have a heart that is steadfast toward God? Write a prayer of commitment below.

Watch this chapter's video teaching at
www.rhondastoppe.com/books/moms-raising-sons-to-be-men.

CHAPTER 2

GOD CHOSE *YOU* TO BE HIS MOM

Your Place in History

Back when I was having my children, ultrasounds were not routinely performed. The first and only time I was given the opportunity to see one of my babies within my womb was when I was pregnant with my second child.

An unexpected outpouring of emotions washed over me as I studied that sweet little profile. The baby had a turned-up nose and chubby little cheeks like its big sister. It held up a tiny thumb ready to be placed into its mouth. Psalm 139:13-16 flooded my thoughts as I cherished my first glimpse of my precious baby, a son:

> You formed my inward parts;
> You covered me in my mother's womb.
> I will praise You, for I am fearfully and wonderfully made;
> Marvelous are Your works,
> And that my soul knows very well.
> My frame was not hidden from You,
> When I was made in secret...
> Your eyes saw my substance, being yet unformed.

And in Your book they all were written,
The days fashioned for me,
When as yet there were none of them.

When I left the doctor's office that day, I contemplated the marvelous truth that *God Himself was knitting my son together within my womb,* and He had plans for my son's future. Just as God had written in His book of remembrance all the days He had "fashioned" for David, He wrote the days determined for my son as well.

The idea that God had specific intentions for my little one's life was too extraordinary to fathom. I could thoroughly relate to David's response in Psalm 139:6: "Such knowledge is too wonderful for me; it is high, I cannot attain it." Just as the Lord had sovereignly chosen to use David's mother in His plan to train up a godly king, He had chosen to involve me in developing the character of my son.

Here is some exciting news: God chose *you* as the mother of your son. Before the very foundation of this world, the Creator knew your name *and* He knew your son's name. God wrote the number of your days and those of your son's in His book of remembrance. And He ordained the generation in which you and your son would live.

As I ponder these awesome truths, my heart cries out with David the psalmist: "When I consider Your heavens, the work of Your fingers, the moon and the stars, which You have ordained, what is man that You are mindful of him, and the son of man that You visit him?" (Psalm 8:3-4).

I can hardly contain my excitement as I read that! Our sovereign God leaves nothing to chance. Everything He does is purposeful and thought-out. He had you in mind when He assigned your son to you. He planned that you would join Him in the glorious work of raising your son to be a godly man.

As I waited for my son's birth, I could not help but wonder what the Lord would accomplish through him. I thought, *How can I best equip myself to be his mother?*

Your Choices Today Determine Who You Are Tomorrow

How many choices do you think you make in a day? Some decisions are so routine that it does not even seem like you are making choices. For example, I have coffee every morning. Lots and lots of coffee. Is that a choice? I guess so. Making coffee has become such a part of my morning that almost without thinking I wake up, stumble to the coffee maker, and begin my ritual of measuring out the coffee beans. It's funny—I know the exact amount of beans to pour out, and yet I still measure them out every time as though it were rocket science.

Each morning, with cup in hand, my day begins. And I make choice after choice as I work through the day—and so do you. In the 18 years that my husband, Steve, was in youth ministry, he repeatedly told the kids, "Your choices today determine who you are tomorrow." As we have watched kids from our youth ministry grow up to adulthood, Steve's words have proven true. A person's choices definitely influence their character and the direction they take in life.

Some choices are of little consequence, while others will change your future forever and will greatly influence your son. As you walk along the path of this life, do you involve the Lord in the choices you make? Rather than carelessly making each decision, do you make an effort to prepare yourself to identify and follow the Lord's leading? Have you ever considered that your choices—both big and small— are a reflection of who you are?

It is God's desire that His children walk so closely to His heart that His guidance would be an ongoing source of courage, comfort, and refuge. When we seek Him at every step of the way, we can know the assurance that we are more likely to make the right kinds of choices in life.

A Decision That Changed Everything

One very normal day, Mary was going about her business. She

couldn't help but smile when she thought of how fortunate she was—betrothed to the kindest man she had ever known. Oh, what a blessed future lay ahead of them! I can only speculate on the thoughts that Mary, the mother of Jesus, may have had leading up to her encounter with the angel Gabriel. The Bible doesn't tell us her age, but we do know she was young. In ancient Israel, it was a cultural norm for a young virgin to be betrothed when she began to menstruate. If that were the case for Mary, then it is quite possible she would have been a young teenager at the time we first meet her in Scripture.

I have helped my two daughters and one daughter-in-law plan their weddings. Anyone who has been a part of such a glorious experience knows that from the time the engagement ring is placed on a young bride's finger until the day she walks down the aisle, her mind is filled with excitement and decisions as she plans the blessed day. Mary would have been just like any other bride—or was she?

Because God chose Mary to be the mother of Jesus, don't you think it's worthwhile to see what we can learn about her character? What moved God to entrust Mary with the ministry of being the mother of His only begotten Son? The Bible reveals many things about this young woman; let's look at some of her qualities and see how we can apply them to our own lives.

Mary was a virgin. In obedience to God's law, Mary had kept herself sexually pure. Several hundred years earlier, the Lord had prophesied through Isaiah that a virgin would conceive the promised Messiah. Mary's purity made her a woman the Lord could use to accomplish His great plan. Have you ever considered that immorality could keep you from being a vessel of honor for the Master's use?

In today's culture, there is a regrettable tolerance for sexual promiscuity. I have met single mothers who profess to be Christians yet were actively involved in intimate relationships that did not honor or obey God. And I've met married women who regularly view pornography or, on social media, engage in emotional affairs. Their consciences were seared by the sinful choices they had made. This lifestyle steals their passion for Christ so that they become apathetic in service to Him.

A mother who chooses to be promiscuous can have a negative influence upon her son's personal purity. What's more, a Christian mother who dishonors the Lord by flirting, engaging in emotional affairs, or having sex outside of marriage *cannot* be led by the Spirit. Galatians 5:16 makes this clear for Christians: "Walk in the Spirit, and you shall not fulfill the lust of the flesh." In other words, we cannot do both at the same time. Either we are led by the Spirit, or we aren't. If you are not led by the Spirit, your best efforts to train your son will be just that—*your* best efforts rather than God working through you. Be warned, my friend: Spiritual apathy will cause your son to reject your faith.

Mary was highly favored of God. Luke 1:28 tells us that, in the middle of what otherwise had been an ordinary day, the angel Gabriel appeared to Mary and said, "Rejoice, highly favored one, the Lord is with you; blessed are you among women!" As Gabriel continued to share about God's plan for Mary to conceive the very Son of God, he said, "Do not be afraid, Mary, for you have found favor with God" (verse 30). Can you imagine how it would feel if God called you highly favored? *Highly favored* literally means "full of grace."

Mary had received grace from God. This is the same grace that God avails to you and me through a personal relationship with Jesus Christ. His amazing grace makes it possible for sinners to be accepted and beloved by the Lord. God doesn't expect you to be perfect to accomplish His plans through your life. Through Christ's free gift of salvation, He provides a way for you to be covered with His grace so that you, too, can be highly favored for His service.

Mary was a woman who prayed. Luke 1:46-55 records Mary's prayer to the Lord, which is known as Mary's Magnificat. Her words reveal that she was quite comfortable expressing her heart to the

Lord. Prayer is just that—expressing your heart to God. If you are not a person who prays, let me give you one profound piece of advice—pray!

Don't worry about what to say; just speak out loud to the Lord. He is not looking for eloquent words; He simply wants you to pour out your heart to Him and express your love and worship for Him.

For years I struggled with the fact my thoughts would wander while I prayed. Then I learned a valuable principle that helped me enormously—that of talking out loud when I pray. If you're like me, trying to hold a conversation with God in your mind tends to be a struggle. But if you communicate with the Lord the way that you communicate with others, you may find—as I did—that it is a natural and comfortable experience. I even use my hands when I speak—you should see me when I am talking to the Lord! If someone were to walk into the room during my prayer time, I am quite sure they would think I had lost my mind.

Mary knew her purpose. In the very first line of her prayer, Mary revealed her heart: "My soul magnifies the Lord" (verse 46). To *magnify* means "to enlarge, to declare, or to show great." In that brief statement Mary conveyed that she understood her purpose in life was to bring glory to her God. Her obedience to Him would do just that.

Mary knew God as her Savior. In Luke 1:47, Mary referred to God as her Savior. That demonstrated she recognized her need of a Savior. As John MacArthur notes, "She employed language typical of someone whose only hope for salvation is divine grace."[1]

Just as Mary needed a Savior, so you and I are in need of a Savior. A relationship with Jesus Christ is our only hope of salvation.

Mary was humble. Mary's humility was made evident by how she referred to herself in her prayer: "He has regarded the lowly state of His maidservant" (Luke 1:48). Throughout history God has used meek people mightily—humble servants who learned to rely upon His strength.

Mary inquired of the Lord. When Gabriel announced that Mary would give birth to the Son of God, she respectfully asked, "How can this be, since I do not know a man?" (Luke 1:34). We shouldn't interpret her question to mean she didn't believe what Gabriel had told her. Rather, "her question was borne out of wonder, not doubt, nor disbelief."[2] When faced with a monumental situation, Mary wisely directed her inquiries to the messenger of God.

Mary was courageous. Luke 1:29 reveals Mary's immediate response to this strange news: "She was troubled at his saying." How surreal this moment must have been for her. Imagine the thoughts that may have gone through her mind. *How is this possible? Will Joseph believe me? What will my parents think?*

With no witnesses to vouch for this encounter with Gabriel, Mary would likely have wondered if anyone would believe her. The Law of Moses made provision for Joseph to break off their engagement on account of her pregnancy, and by law she could be stoned to death as an adulteress.

Though Mary faced painful losses, in her moment of decision she courageously presented herself as the maidservant of the Lord and surrendered to His plan for her.

Mary knew the Word of God. I am amazed at how quickly Mary chose to obey the Lord. What equipped this young girl to cast aside the safety of her neat and orderly life in exchange for obedience to God? Mary and most other Jewish maidens would have known Isaiah's prophecy that one day a virgin would conceive and bear a son (Isaiah 7:14). Mary's ability to recognize God's calling would likely have come from her knowledge of Scripture.

As a mother, if you want your decisions to be directed by the Lord, you must be familiar with His Word. It is essential that you determine to be a woman who studies the Bible so you develop the courage to follow the Lord's leading—for it is a lamp to your feet and a light to your path (Psalm 119:105).

God, through His Word, has established the way for His people to find direction. It has never been the Lord's intent for you to wait until you are facing a decision before you open the Bible, close your eyes, and randomly point to a verse for His guidance—as if you were in some cosmic game show. The Lord expects His children to daily transform their thoughts by meditating upon and studying His Word so they will think with the mind of Christ. In so doing, they will view life and its decisions with His perspective rather than their own. The Word of God will provide the direction you need to follow Christ no matter the cost. When faced with a difficult choice, are you prepared to recognize and submit to the Lord's leading, or are you tempted to play it safe?

Mary chose to do God's will. When the all-knowing Father chose Mary to be the virgin who would carry His Son, He understood the personal sacrifice Mary would be making. In His kindness, the Lord sent the angel Gabriel that day not only to proclaim the message about her pregnancy, but also to give her the courage to submit to His perfect plan.

When Mary respectfully asked how it would be possible for her to conceive as a virgin, Gabriel did not chastise her. Rather, he told her that her cousin Elizabeth, who was old and barren, had conceived. He then said, "With God nothing will be impossible" (Luke 1:37). Evidently those were the exact words Mary needed to hear, for she responded, "Behold the maidservant of the Lord! Let it be to me according to your word" (Luke 1:38).

When faced with a difficult choice, are you prepared to recognize and submit to the Lord's leading, or are you tempted to play it safe?

That it seemed impossible she could become pregnant without knowing a man did not matter to Mary. Nor was she swayed by what her beloved Joseph might think. She would leave that to the Lord. It seemed to be a natural response for this teenage girl to trust God completely. Even the fear of what others would think could not keep this courageous teen from obeying her Lord. The Word of God had prepared her grace-filled heart so that she could not resist His leading.

What if Mary had pulled out her legal-sized tablet and began writing a pros-and-cons list of how this decision would impact her world? What might she have missed if she had chosen to play it safe?

The Temptation to Play It Safe

When a church in California offered my husband, Steve, a pastoral position, we prayed for several months about the decision. We loved our church in Austin. Leaving Texas would be a heartbreaking sacrifice.

My poor husband endured my need to continually talk through every aspect of the decision. One day we dropped the children off at school, returned home to put on a pot of coffee, and he said, "We will talk about this as long as you need today, but then we are not going to talk about it anymore. We are going to pray and wait on the Lord." Evidently I'd been driving him a bit crazy by constantly analyzing the options. Do you do that?

I took out my notepad and made two columns, labeling one *pros* and the other *cons*. We talked that entire day. As we logically evaluated the options, the list without a doubt showed it was better to stay in Texas. But the very moment we leaned toward the safe decision, both our hearts were gripped by the Holy Spirit.

Almost immediately the Lord brought to mind how the Ephesians had wept with the apostle Paul when he left their church (Acts 20:17–21:14). Even though they all were deeply sorrowful, Paul knew that God was leading him to Jerusalem. The Scriptures reveal to us how difficult this decision was for Paul. He said to them, "What do you mean by weeping and breaking my heart? For I am ready not only to be bound, but also to die at Jerusalem for the name of the Lord Jesus" (Acts 21:13).

As Steve and I read the Bible, the Lord reminded us that even though leaving the church we loved so dearly would be difficult, we could not be led by our emotions. It was His plan for us to go; we absolutely could not resist His leading. Though it would break our hearts, we knew we had to trust the Lord. We packed up our things and tearfully drove to California. It was one of the hardest things we have ever had to do. But now, looking back 20 years later, we clearly see God's plan in bringing us back to California.

It's Not All About You

Often the method Christians employ as they make major decisions is to walk through the doors of least resistance. They turn away from anything that is difficult or causes anxiety, concluding that they had "no peace."

In this feeling-based process there is a danger that we will be led by our emotions rather than by the Holy Spirit. If you are certain you are living in obedience to God's Word, relying on a sense of peace is part of the process of good decision making. But if peace is your sole criterion for how you make decisions, it may keep you from stepping out in faith.

If in your parenting you always follow the path that seems to require the least sacrifice, you may give your son the impression that God would never ask him to do anything that is hard or uncomfortable. Does your example teach your son to courageously follow the Lord's leading?

During our drive out to California, everything that could go wrong did. When we arrived, exhausted and bewildered by how rough our trip had been, our home was not ready. To add to the stress, it was two days before Christmas. If we were looking for closed doors, we could have found several. We prayed, "Lord, if You just give us the word, we will turn around and go right back to Texas." But amid all our problems, God gave us a quiet confidence that we were exactly where He wanted us. In spite of the difficulties, His Spirit led us onward.

At the time of this writing, Steve and I have been serving this same church in California for 23 years. Without question, it has been a wonderful time of ministry blessed of the Lord. Looking back, we can see that in leading us to California, the move was much more than God's plan for us. It was also His preparation for the futures and ministries of our children. The Lord has developed in each of them the courage to follow wherever He may lead.

Each time that the Lord directs our younger son to a new place of ministry, I watch him struggle with the sacrifice of forsaking the familiar for the unknown. As he wrestles with the decision, he invariably steps out in faith—sometimes through tears, but always in obedience. I cannot help but believe that as he grew up watching the Lord faithfully lead our family, he has learned the importance of having the courage to follow Christ—even when the decision is a difficult one.

Your Life Matters to God

In the same way that God specifically chose to accomplish His plan through Mary in her generation, He has placed you on earth in this generation to fulfill His purposes through your obedience. In Christ you are significant, and so is your son. How can you know this?

- God knows you both intimately—you are not just a face in the crowd (Psalm 139:1-4).

- God loves you, and your son, more than you can imagine (Ephesians 2:4-5, 17-19).

- You are a "temple of the living God" (2 Corinthians 6:16).

- God chose you to be His child (2 Corinthians 6:18; Ephesians 1:4-6).

- God is watchful over your every trial and opportunity (Psalm 34:15).

- God will direct your steps (Psalm 32:8; Jeremiah 10:23).

- God has a specific purpose for your life—and your son's (Jeremiah 29:11).

From my own upbringing I can attest to the longing children have to feel significant. When I came to know my worth in Christ's love for me, I discovered satisfaction and purpose. However, my sister, who rejected the gospel, spent her life seeking significance in her successes. She became a film producer and a millionaire, yet her longing for purpose was never satisfied by her worldly pursuits. Sadly, her life ended tragically. She never knew that the secret to her success would have been found in submission to the God who loved her so much He sent His Son to purchase her for His treasure.

Learning how much God values you is greater than any treasure this world can offer. And teaching your son how to find his significance in his relationship with the Lord will be one of the greatest gifts you can give him. When you find your worth in Christ's love and purpose for your life, your example can teach your children to do the same.

Just like Mary, Jesus's mother, each of us is faced with choices in life. As mothers, our decisions will influence the next generation. If we as moms do not prepare ourselves to live courageous, obedient lives, we are in danger of raising sons who are more interested in living for the comforts and accomplishments of this world than in obedience to the Lord's leading.

God has accomplished incredible things through women who have boldly chosen to follow His call—even when doing so required great personal sacrifice. And generations of godly men have testified of their courageous mothers who chose to follow the Lord and the powerful effect it had upon them. Wouldn't you like that to be true about you as a mother? God has an ideal plan for you and for your son. To dwell in obedience to His will is to exist beyond the average, status-quo life. Are you willing to rise above the mundane and allow the Lord to accomplish amazing things through you— and your son?

THINKING IT THROUGH

Read Psalm 139. How will understanding that God formed your son and knows him intimately influence the way you raise your son?

Write out and memorize 1 Corinthians 2:9.

LIVING IT OUT

Are you willing to become a woman who loves and obeys the Lord's leading above all else? List two or three specific ways you will prepare yourself to better follow the Lord.

Watch this chapter's video teaching at
www.rhondastoppe.com/books/moms-raising-sons-to-be-men.

CHAPTER 3

EXCHANGING YOUR DREAMS FOR GOD'S PLANS

Motives That Matter

Can you even begin to imagine the hopes and dreams that Mary would have held for her son, Jesus? As she studied His precious little face, did she play over in her mind what the angel Gabriel had spoken to her so many months before?

Gabriel had told Mary that the child born to her would be the Holy One, the Son of God. The shepherds, who came to see Jesus, said the angels had told them that the child's birth would bring good tidings of great joy to all people—He was the promised Savior, Christ the Lord. And the wise men who had come to see Him had called Jesus the "King of the Jews" (Matthew 2:2).

How exciting it must have been for Mary to hear about her son's future. The Bible says this young mother pondered all these things in her heart (Luke 2:19). I wonder if she quietly entertained visions of her son as a great king seated upon His throne, ruling over Israel.

I'm not sure that I would have been as discreet and humble as

Mary. In this age of social networking, I can only imagine how I might have abused that medium to boast about how special my son was. How do you think you would have responded to such glorious news about your son's future?

When Jesus was eight days old, Mary and Joseph followed Jewish custom and took Him to Jerusalem to be circumcised. There they were met by an older man named Simeon, who took the little baby into his arms and rejoiced as he announced that in Jesus, the Lord had allowed him to see God's salvation. He proclaimed that Jesus would be a light of revelation to the Gentiles, and the glory of the Lord's people Israel (Luke 2:25-32). What a magnificent announcement! Surely Simeon's words would have confirmed the hopes and dreams Mary held in her heart for her baby boy.

Simeon then turned to Mary and said, "Behold, this Child is destined for the fall and rising of many in Israel, and for a sign which will be spoken against (yes, a sword will pierce through your own soul also), that thoughts of many hearts may be revealed" (Luke 2:34-35).

Simeon's statement was "undoubtedly a reference to the personal grief Mary would endure when she watched her own Son die in agony (John 19:25)."[1] It was as if God was preparing His servant Mary for the grief she would one day endure. Maybe *her* dreams for her son were not exactly what God had in store for Him.

Thirty-three years later, when Mary was standing at the foot of the cross, did she recall Simeon's words? Did remembering his prophecy give Mary confidence in the Lord's sovereignty? Did it give her courage to know that God had sent the elderly man to help prepare her for that awful day?

And what went through Mary's mind during the days leading up to Jesus's death? She would certainly have heard the crowd turn from shouting, "Blessed is He who comes in the name of the Lord" to "Crucify Him!" Was it a struggle for her to exchange the dreams she may have had for Jesus and replace them with God's plans?

In a Moment Everything Changed

My son Brandon was six years old the night he had his first seizure. We had just moved to Austin, Texas. My husband, Steve, had flown back to California to pick up one of our vehicles, and he was in the midst of an all-night drive back to Texas.

Our daughter, Kayla, then four years old, had asked Brandon to sleep on the bottom bunk of her bed because she was still adjusting to her new room. At about 11:00 p.m., I was downstairs when Kayla screamed, "Something's wrong with Brandon!"

I rushed upstairs to find Brandon on the floor. His head was up against the wall with his neck bent severely, and his hands were twisted. He was having a seizure. My first thought was that he had somehow fallen off the top bunk and broken his neck. Kayla assured me that nothing like that had happened. She had heard him make a gurgling sound, looked over, and seen him writhing on the floor.

I called 911. Meredith, my 12-year-old daughter, met the police officer at the door and brought him upstairs. The paramedics came as well as a helicopter, and Brandon was still seizing. For half an hour, my precious boy convulsed in my arms.

When the seizure finally ended, Brandon was unconscious, blue, and not breathing. The paramedics were just about to do a tracheotomy when Brandon finally gasped for air. They hurried Brandon to the helicopter and flew away.

As I stood in the street watching the helicopter rush Brandon to the hospital, I thought, *I don't even know where the hospital is.* How very alone I felt at that moment! I remember thinking, *Why would the Lord allow this to happen now when all of our church family is back in California—and Steve is out of town?* I took a moment to call my friend Shellie in California, and I asked her to pray and to call others to pray for Brandon.

Somewhere in the chaos, my father arrived. As he drove me to the hospital, I pleaded with God not to take Brandon from me.

Then I became less frightened that Brandon might die, and more concerned that the amount of time he had gone without oxygen might have caused brain damage. The last I had seen Brandon, he was talking—but not like the bright, intelligent six-year-old he had been. He was talking baby talk, not at all articulate.

When we arrived at the hospital I was greeted by my bright-eyed little boy, who cried out, "Momma, I rode in a helicopter!" I was so relieved; I was convinced that my son was going to be just fine. I thought, *Praise the Lord—He answered our prayers!*

Steve arrived at the hospital early that morning. Together we thanked God for sparing our son. We prayed for the Lord's will to be done while Brandon remained in the hospital for a series of tests. (In my heart I was convinced that the seizure was a one-time thing.)

A week later the phone call came. The test results revealed that Brandon had severe seizure activity taking place in his brain. Our little boy had epilepsy. I thought, *How is this possible? He is so normal. It was just one seizure. Surely there won't be another.*

Another did come, and another, and another. While the neurologist worked to determine the medications that would help stop or at least minimize the seizures, Brandon spent the next three months sleeping on the floor in our bedroom. I lay on my stomach with my arm dangled over the edge of the bed, and Brandon would hold my hand as he fell asleep. Many times he would clutch my hand and cry out, "Mommy!" and have a seizure.

I was afraid for Brandon to sleep anywhere else. If I could not hear the seizure, he would be all alone through the scary experience—and he could even stop breathing. All through this trying time, I found myself fretting over what could have happened to Brandon the night he had his first seizure. *What if he had not been sleeping in Kayla's room that night? I would not have heard him. He probably would have died.*

Steve worked diligently to remind me not to coddle Brandon because of my fears. He wanted our son to have the opportunity to be as normal as any other little boy in spite of his condition. In all this, God faithfully gave me glimpses of His sovereign care. It was *His* protective hand, not mine, that had designed for Brandon to sleep in Kayla's room that night. The Lord had worked to preserve Brandon's life.

Daily I wrestled with my thoughts of fear and disappointment. How had this become our life? All had been so normal—but in a moment, everything changed. The hopes we'd had for our son's future were suddenly lost in a haze of doctor's visits, seizures, and medications.

I do not have the words to describe how helpless my husband and I felt each time Brandon had a seizure. I knew I needed to trust the Lord, but with each seizure came new fear and sorrow.

Over the next several years, Brandon's medications worked to keep his seizures to a minimum. However, the medications were strong, and they sedated our poor son terribly. His personality was definitely altered by the drugs, and his social development was affected as well. He was sleepy and quiet much of the time.

At school, Brandon's teachers modified his assignments. The phrase *special ed*, used casually by the school administrators, pierced my heart. My bright and articulate little man became a shadow of who he had been. Once very active, Brandon now preferred to stay inside. Any athletic aspirations that his father and I had for him were now lost in lethargy. Each seizure was a painful reminder that our son's condition was not getting any better. I knew from Romans 8:28 that God causes all things to work together for good, but as I searched to find any good in the situation, I became less convinced that was possible—to the point where I was tempted to walk away from ministry. But God drew me back when He impressed upon my heart: "In everything give thanks; for this is the will of God in Christ Jesus for you" (1 Thessalonians 5:18). I couldn't imagine how I could be thankful for my son's seizures. But I decided to say "thank You" with my mouth, while asking God to change my heart.

God's Ways Are Not Ours

As life took on a new kind of normal, we adapted to Brandon's condition. In the midst of the adjustment, Steve and another pastor started a new church.

We rented a school gymnasium for the Sunday services, and every other activity took place in our home. Two hundred teenagers met at our house every Wednesday night. After they left, we held late-night band practice in our dining room to rehearse the worship music for church.

Brandon loved the music. Each week during rehearsal he would plant himself in the room, studying the drummer one week, the guitarist the next, and the pianist the next. Anything the musicians would teach Brandon he would diligently practice until the next week's rehearsal, during which he would excitedly show them what he had mastered.

It quickly became apparent that music was Brandon's passion. He took guitar lessons. He loved playing the guitar and would practice for hours on end. He also learned to play the drums and the piano. In school Brandon took saxophone lessons, and soon became first chair. Although Brandon's medication made him less than social with children his own age, he loved the older boys in our youth group, and they were great with him. It didn't take long for them to realize that if they invited Brandon to play music with them, they would have access to all the sound equipment in our dining room. They frequently played with Brandon, and his skills grew at an amazing rate.

Over the next four years we watched Brandon develop an incredible talent as a musician. As the Lord molded his love for music, it gradually began to dawn on us that God was preparing Brandon to accomplish *His* dreams for Brandon *His* way.

My plan had been to hear the crowd glory in my son's accomplishment as Brandon passed the football, sunk a basket, or knocked one out of the park. God's plan was to raise up our son to bring the crowd to glory in *His* Son's accomplishments—through worship.

My motive was to hear others praise the abilities of *my* son. God's motive was, through Brandon, to lead many to praise *His* Son.

Brandon grew up to tour with well-known Christian musicians. Today, he's an accomplished worship pastor in California. And these days Brandon appears with me on radio and TV interviews, at homeschool conventions, and at mother-son events. I can say with absolute confidence and assurance that Brandon's epilepsy was God's way of preparing him for service to Him.

And now, our niece Taylor experiences epileptic seizures so debilitating she had to resign from her career as hairstylist. Although it has been painful to watch Taylor battle her seizures, we've also observed how God has used her frailty to bring Taylor to repentance and wholehearted devotion to Christ. Taylor says, "I know God used my seizures to bring me to salvation."

Taylor and I have founded an online Christian support community called Seize His Way. Her zeal to encourage others to trust Christ amid their storm is incredible evidence of how God is using Taylor in her weakness for His glory.

Remember, when your kids endure struggles, sometimes the trial is not about you. Perhaps it's about God equipping them for His kingdom purpose in their lives.

Fishermen or Fishers of Men

Salome was the mother of James and John—two of Jesus's disciples. Early on in Jesus's public ministry, the two brothers left their father's successful fishing business to follow the Teacher.

I wonder how Salome and Zebedee took the news when James and John left home to become Jesus's disciples. Had she and her husband wasted all their energy training their boys to take over the family trade? Were their dreams dashed as their sons proclaimed they would no longer be fishermen but fishers of men? What would people think now that both of their boys were following this controversial prophet?

Have you ever considered that the plans the Lord has for your son may not look like success in the eyes of those who are watching? While it is vital to prepare your son to work hard, you must not minimize the importance of equipping him to recognize and follow God's call. You must take great care not to allow the treasures of this life to seduce you away from teaching your son that the priority of life is to make great the name of the Lord, not to make a name for himself.

It has been a satisfying experience to celebrate with my sons over their many achievements. However, I cannot begin to imagine how much more fulfilling it will be to rejoice in heaven with them when Jesus says, "Well done, good and faithful servant." Never be more concerned about training your son for a career and financial success than about preparing him for what the Lord will accomplish through him. No earthly trophy could ever compare to the eternal rewards that the Lord will give to your son if he faithfully serves Him. Consider the joy your son will experience in heaven if he is one day surrounded by people who are there because of his faithful witness on behalf of the Lord.

In Matthew 27:56, Salome is listed as one of the many women who followed and ministered to Jesus. So it is safe to conclude that at some point the two brothers would have rejoiced in their mother's conversion.

Jesus called James and John the "Sons of Thunder," likely referring to their intense and boisterous personalities. Don't you just love to be around people like that when something wonderful happens? I like to imagine a great outburst of celebration, along with crushing hugs from her exuberant sons, as Salome put her trust in Jesus.

Salome's decision to become a follower of Christ would likely have helped her understand why her boys left their promising careers in the family fishing business. Once possibly disappointed by their decision, she became a confident supporter of her sons, who were counted among those in the close inner circle of the Messiah, the Promised One of Israel.

One day when Jesus was at the height of His popularity, James, John, and their mother, Salome, became a bit distracted by the perceived success of His ministry. Jesus had spoken of the throne, from which He would one day reign (Matthew 19:27-28), and the two brothers began to discuss with each other their desire to sit on either side of Jesus when He was made king. With the throngs of followers growing ever larger, they likely thought it was just a matter of time before that event took place.

Upon evaluating all of this, Momma Salome determined that her boys deserved those seats of honor. She decided it was time to pull a few strings to get James and John what they wanted. And her boys did not try to stop her. Salome knelt before Jesus and said, "Grant that these two sons of mine may sit, one on Your right hand and the other on the left, in Your kingdom" (Matthew 20:21).

How did Jesus respond? He told Salome she had no idea what she was requesting. Jesus knew He would soon die upon the cross, and that Salome was unwittingly requesting her sons "drink the cup" of suffering Jesus was about to drink.

When the other disciples heard about the request, they were greatly displeased with the two brothers. And it wasn't because any of the other disciples were humbler; they felt they deserved the two seats of honor as well! Salome's effort to control the outcome had caused the other disciples to become upset with her boys. Her manipulative scheme sowed seeds of discord, jealousy, and competition within the group. In Matthew 20:27-28, Jesus addressed the very heart of their problem—pride. He said, "Whoever desires to be first among you, let him be your slave—just as the Son of Man did not come to be served, but to serve, and to give His life a ransom for many." Jesus convicted the disciples of their prideful ways and redirected their thoughts. For them to display such arrogance over who was worthiest to sit in the seats of honor was not a good thing before a watching world.

Motivate, Don't Manipulate

What lessons can we learn from Salome?

Don't attempt to control circumstances. You can do great damage if you are constantly meddling and pushing for your son's advancement. It is better and more productive for you to help your son recognize opportunities and give him the encouragement he needs to pursue them on his own. Rather than try to control events to promote your son's success, turn the control over to Christ, who is able to work all things together for good (Romans 8:28).

Don't manipulate others to gain favor. Some mothers, with the motive of gaining favor or position for their son, become the room-mother in the classroom, bake cookies for the coach, or pursue a friendship with an authority figure. Usually it doesn't take long to discern the mother's motives. This often has a negative influence upon the unity of the group, stirring feelings of jealousy or rivalry. A mother's conniving actions may also teach her son to manipulate people to get what he wants. Kids are quick to pick up on what their parents are doing. Assisting a leader is a wonderful thing, but not if it's done with the wrong motive.

Wait on the Lord. As a mother, learn to wait for the Lord to open opportunities for your son. Trust in God's sovereignty, and let Him make things happen. Your son will learn, from watching you, how he should live his life. By your example, lead your son down a path that patiently waits on Christ. Remind him that "a man's heart plans his way, but the LORD directs his steps" (Proverbs 16:9).

Teach your son to pursue Christ. Avoid using schemes to achieve a favorable outcome. Guard yourself from pursuing the prize of personal advancement by keeping your eyes on the Prize—Jesus Christ (Philippians 3:14). Remind your son that serving Him well is the greatest motivation in life.

Teach humility by example. James 4:6 teaches that God actively "resists the proud." No success achieved through vain aspiration will ever be blessed of the Lord. There is failure in the victory if it is acquired through prideful ambition. Numbers 12:3 describes Moses as "very humble, more than all men who were on the face of the earth." Oh, what a glorious compliment from the Lord! God has influenced thousands of generations through the humble life of His servant Moses. Can you imagine what great things the Lord could do through your son if you teach him the value of humility?

> Rather than try to control events to promote your son's success, turn the control over to Christ, who is able to work all things together for good.

Pray for God to lead and direct your son. Prayer is one of the greatest contributions you can make toward your son's success. Remember, Salome did not clearly understand God's plan for her sons. Likewise, you cannot comprehend God's plan for your son through your own wisdom. So ask God to help you pray according to His will—and not your own.

The Motivation That Matters

No matter our actions, it's vital that our motivation be to bring glory to God. At the foot of the cross, whatever dreams Mary may have had for Jesus were surrendered for God's plans. Salome learned that pushing James and John to have a favored position in the kingdom was for her own glory, not the Lord's. The Lord sovereignly ordained that each of these women would be the mother of their son. He used them as instruments to prepare their sons for His service, for His glory. In the same way, God the Father has ordained for you to be the mother who will invest in the life of your son and equip him to glorify Him.

At this moment Mary and Salome have no regrets. They are standing in heaven, rejoicing together around the throne of God.

The heavenly reward these women will receive because of their obedience to God can never compare to anything they may have sacrificed during their time on earth. If these women could speak to us, I am confident they would cheer us on to become mothers who surrender our earthly dreams for our sons and replace them with the Lord's divine plans.

Can you picture what it will be like when at last you enter into the very presence of Almighty God? How glorious it will be when the Lord welcomes you into heaven. But how much *more* glorious it will be on the day when, in heaven, you see the Lord look to your son and say, "Well done, good and faithful servant"!

THINKING IT THROUGH

Read Mark 8:34-36. Write in your own words Jesus's message to anyone who will follow Him.

In a brief moment, everything can change—just as it did the night my son Brandon had his first seizure. What encouragement can you glean from Romans 8:28 for those times when life suddenly becomes difficult?

LIVING IT OUT

Do you believe that God answers the prayers of mothers? Write out some specific prayer requests you will commit to praying on behalf of your son.

Watch this chapter's video teaching at
www.rhondastoppe.com/books/moms-raising-sons-to-be-men.

CHAPTER 4

ONE ACT IMPACTS GENERATIONS

Living Beyond the Immediate

Sixty years ago my husband's aunt was surprised when she gave birth to twins. Can you imagine the shock? Because she had not had months to ponder clever names for *two* babies instead of one, she instinctively relied on a familiar nursery rhyme and named them Jack and Jill. These days, however, technology has made it quite rare for mothers to be surprised by a multiple-birth pregnancy, allowing them sufficient time to prepare for the demands of caring for two or more babies.

In Genesis 25:23, when Rebekah found out she was carrying twin boys, she received the announcement not from her doctor, but from the Lord Himself. Scripture tells us that while Rebekah was still pregnant, the Lord informed her that the older twin, Esau, would one day serve Jacob, the younger twin.

As the years passed, the boys grew into men. When their aged father, Isaac, prepared to pass on the blessing of birthright to Esau, Rebekah devised a scheme by which Jacob could steal the heritage from his older brother, the legal heir. Rebekah's fear that Jacob would not receive the inheritance of the firstborn kept her from waiting on God to bring about His perfect will. When Rebekah set out to "help God" accomplish what He had promised for Jacob, the consequences for her sinful deception were painful, and more far-reaching than she could have imagined.

With good intentions, have you ever tried to manipulate circumstances and people only to find that your plan blew up in your face? When Esau learned that Jacob had stolen his blessing, he was so angry that he vowed to kill his younger brother. Jacob had to flee from home in fear of his life. As it turned out, Rebekah would never see Jacob again, and he would not return to his homeland for another 40 years. Can you imagine what painful regret must have burdened Rebekah's heart as she watched her precious Jacob leave home? How Rebekah must have longed to take back her sinful actions of that dreadful day!

Your Agenda Versus God's Agenda

God had given Rebekah a glimpse of His great plan for Jacob. Rather than prayerfully waiting upon the Lord to accomplish His perfect will, Rebekah developed her own ideas of how to ensure a successful future for Jacob.

As your son grows up, God may give you glimpses of your boy's strengths. In the course of discovering your son's abilities, don't become so excited by his potential that you push rather than guide him. While it is important for you to celebrate your son's strong points, you need to make sure you balance your encouraging words with respect for God's authority. Rather than promoting your personal agenda, submit to God's plans, and let Him work out your son's future in His way and time.

How can you discern whether your plans are godly? One good question to ask yourself is this: Will this plan draw other people's attention to me and my son, or will it bring honor to the Lord? An insidious temptation we as mothers face is to raise our sons for our own distinction rather than for the esteem of the Lord. As you contemplate how to support your son's achievements, make it a habit to prayerfully evaluate your motives.

In Isaiah 43:7, God said He created people for His glory. One who lives for the sole purpose of glorifying God is one whose life will be successful and satisfying. Will you determine to be more concerned about the reputation of Christ reflected in you and your son than in your own standing as a mother?

The Lord knows how He plans to accomplish His purposes through your son. That's why pressing ahead of God with any of your own schemes is unwise. Examining your personal motives is a difficult and ever-changing task. Through consistent prayer and the reading of Scripture, the Holy Spirit will help you discern your motives. No other resource can better help you discover your motivations than the Word of God, because it "is living and powerful…and is a discerner of the thoughts and intents of the heart" (Hebrews 4:12).

Learning from Others' Mistakes

I am extremely grateful for the women in my life who, through their examples, have taught me how to be a godly mother. I have learned valuable lessons from them; they have made themselves vulnerable to me and humbly taught me from their errors. And today, when I teach other women, my teaching is most passionate when I caution them from my own regrets.

What can we glean from Rebekah's mistakes? Let's take a look:

Don't obsess over the immediate. When Isaac announced it was time for him to pass the birthright on to Esau, Rebekah got caught up in the urgency of the moment, as if it were up to her to set things right before it was too late. I, too, can become so shortsighted by worry over the outcome of a particular circumstance that I forget that God is in control and will take care of things in His time. God's plans go far beyond my immediate concern—and yours.

As it turned out, Isaac didn't die right away. He ended up living for another 43 years, which would have been plenty of time for God to orchestrate what He had promised. If Rebekah had kept her focus on the Lord rather than the circumstance, she likely would have seen God accomplish His miraculous plan according to His schedule, not hers.

If you keep your gaze fixed on the affairs of life, you will ride a roller coaster of emotions. Elation, fear, and all the feelings in between may cause you to respond without depending on God and fully considering the consequences. But when you focus on God, who is the One who knows the times and seasons, you will develop a peaceful confidence no matter what happens. The more disciplined you are in fixing your eyes on Jesus, the more the Lord will teach you to rest in His sovereignty over life's events. And when your son observes your calm assurance in Christ, he will learn—from your example—how to trust the Lord in all the circumstances of his life.

Never play favorites. Jacob enjoyed staying close to home and working with his mother in the kitchen. Esau was a rugged hunter who was often away. Because Jacob spent more time with his mother, it would make sense that he and Rebekah would have a closer bond. Sadly, her preferential treatment drove a wedge between her sons.

While it may be a natural tendency for you as a parent to be drawn to the child who shares your interests or is easier to talk to, playing favorites with your children will fuel disastrous dissension. And if you have a stepchild or an adopted child, you must work extra hard to treat all your children fairly. Partiality is sure to produce volatile consequences.

As you walk in the Spirit—that is, live in submission to His leading in your life—He will equip you to love each of your children with a selfless, genuine love. As your kids observe your wholehearted devotion to each of them, they will gain a total sense of security. Resting in your unconditional love, they will be free from the pressure to measure up in some way or outdo their siblings.

As our kids were growing up, they would regularly ask, "Who's your favorite?" To which I always responded, "Daddy." Steve was also surveyed frequently, and his response was always, "Your momma. You guys are all gonna grow up and leave me. She's gonna be here when you're gone!" Each time our children asked this question, they were exasperated by our answers. They would roll their eyes and groan. However, every time we responded to them with the same answers, their security was reassured. We didn't love one child more than the other, and they knew: *Mommy and Daddy love each other, and none of us is favored more than the other.*

Your children will never feel more secure than when they know that their parents' love is strong. To win your kids to Jesus, one of the greatest witnessing tools you have is the testimony of your loving marriage.

The ends do not justify the means. Rebekah was willing to do whatever was required to make sure Jacob received the birthright that belonged to Esau. She became so preoccupied with making sure Jacob would rule over his older brother that she lost her perspective over right and wrong. Bent on controlling the circumstances, Rebekah deceived her husband, involved Jacob in a manipulative façade, and betrayed her older son. Although her intentions might appear honorable because she wanted to bring about what God had promised, she wrongfully took charge of the situation instead of leaving it in God's hands. Her motives and actions were sinful.

> When your son observes your calm assurance in Christ, he will learn—from your example—how to trust the Lord in all the circumstances of his life.

The "ends justify the means" mentality is a serious problem in our culture. People are guided not by morality, but by the desire to get ahead. Your son is growing up among peers who have been taught they are justified in doing whatever is necessary to gain what they feel they are entitled to.

As a mother, you exert a tremendous amount of influence on how your son will grow up. Your divine calling to the ministry of motherhood is able to impact your children for God's kingdom. And God only knows who He will influence through your child's life. Doesn't that make the mundane daily tasks of motherhood amount to more than just wiping boogers and bums all day long?

As a young mother, I used to pray for God to allow me to do for Him things that would really matter in the world. Little did I realize then how the time I spent guiding my kids' hearts to love and obey Christ would have far-reaching effects upon the next generation. And the same will be true for you! What might our world look like if every mother took seriously the call to instill godly principles and values into her son's character? How differently might your son influence tomorrow's events if you committed to raising him with strong moral qualities? With your words and actions, will you answer that call?

Deception is always wrong. All too often, women withhold information or tell half-truths to their husbands in order to protect their sons from consequence or to bring about favorable results. Scripturally, it is never acceptable to do this. The intimacy and unity of your marriage will suffer if you choose to employ trickery in your relationship. The Bible describes the excellent wife as one whom her husband can trust (Proverbs 31:10-12).

Rebekah's dishonest actions brought sorrowful results, and the same holds true today. Don't fool yourself into thinking you and your family will go unscathed when you resort to lying or wrongdoing.

Your son will learn by your actions. Watch any sitcom about a family on television, and you will likely come across a plot where the mother and children are tricking dad into doing what they want. This is just one of many subtle ways your son is being influenced to believe manipulation is not so bad. Beware that your actions do not reinforce this disrespectful way of thinking.

Remember, your son is learning how to conduct himself in his relationships by watching you. If you say manipulation is wrong but your deeds show otherwise, you will be instructing your son that such behavior is acceptable. So if you practice manipulation, no matter how subtle, don't be shocked when your son attempts to manipulate you!

All through Scripture, we repeatedly see specific details of how God moved in the lives of people for their good and His glory. The Bible records many historical accounts of the Lord's faithfulness to His own, and these examples can help to develop your faith. God's Word will grow your confidence in His character. As you daily equip yourself with truth, fear and worry give way to peace. When I am confused by life's circumstances, the Holy Spirit often reminds me: "The turn of events was from God, that the LORD might fulfill His word" (2 Chronicles 10:15).

While COVID-19 shut down the country and I contemplated the fears of a pandemic, the California wildfires burned out of control on our ranch. We were evacuated for nine days. Shortly after, our grandkids ended up contracting a terrible case of lice—*lice!* (I have raised four children without catching lice, so I thought we had dodged that bullet!) We had to bring our grands to our home when their momma went to the hospital to deliver their new baby sister. You can imagine the heebie-jeebies we all had as we treated, combed, and nitpicked everyone's hair. But through it all, remembering how God turns events for His purposes brought a sense of peace and comfort.

God has the power to turn any situation so that His purpose is fulfilled. The Lord desires that you learn to rely on Him, keeping your eyes on Him and not your circumstances. This, in turn, will influence your son. As a mother, it is not enough for you to tell your son to believe God. He must see you live out your faith. When your actions reflect your confidence in the Lord, your son will learn to trust Him as well.

Will you commit to studying God's Word so you can better understand His ways? The more you read the Bible, the more familiar you will become with God's character and all that He promises to do on your behalf. I make it a habit to read through the Bible every year. As I read, I write "God's ways" in the margin as I see His character revealed in the passage.

As you grow to trust in God's ability to fulfill His plans for your son, you will become confident in His ways rather than your own. You will rest in Him and be free from the compulsion to manipulate people or circumstances. And your son will learn to trust in God's sovereign care as well. In the end, God will be glorified as He carefully orchestrates and fulfills His plan.

One Act Impacts Generations

The deception and dissension within Rebekah's family had been quietly growing over the years. But on that regretful day when Isaac gave the birthright blessing to Jacob, Rebekah's attempt to influence bore disastrous results. For the next four decades, Rebekah's twins were separated by hatred and fear. The descendants of Jacob and Esau became bitter enemies.

Yet God—who is greater than Rebekah's mistake—was able to use Jacob's exile to reveal Himself to Jacob and to develop him into a godly man. Alone, under the stars, the Lord met with Jacob and confirmed His covenant with Jacob and his descendants. At a later time, the Lord changed Jacob's name to Israel. Israel's children would become God's chosen people—the people through whom He would one day bring the promised Messiah, the Savior of the world.

Just as one event can have a negative effect for generations to come, one single act can have a profoundly positive effect upon your descendants as well. So when you walk in obedience to Jesus Christ, you set an example that increases the likelihood of your children doing the same, for God promises to visit righteousness upon the children of those who fear Him (Psalm 103:17).

I can personally attest to the need to remain fully yielded in my relationship with Jesus Christ. For only by His indwelling Spirit and merciful grace have my children grown up loving one another and serving the Lord. I can promise you that parenting in my own strength would certainly have made a mess of my family. When I was raising my children, I made mistakes, and I had to ask my children to forgive me for my selfishness. By the grace of God, they have.

After our third child was born, I experienced postpartum depression. I never had issues with my other pregnancies, so it totally blindsided me. The hormonal imbalances left me overwhelmed and weepy.

Looking back, I recall many days when my six-year-old daughter, Meredith, would arrive home from school. I would turn on a movie for my two-year-old and put the newborn into the arms of my six-year-old so I could go into my room and cry. (Meredith was an extremely responsible big sister. But you're right, leaving the care of my toddler and newborn in the hands of a six-year-old was definitely not the right course of action.)

When I remember those days, I feel shame and sorrow. I long ago asked Meredith to forgive me. And she said, "I don't even remember that, Mom. I just thought it was awesome that I got to hold the new baby!"

Being a Christian will not make you a perfect parent. As if you hadn't figured that out by now, right? No one has ever parented without making any mistakes. However, you can ask God to give you the wisdom you need to train your son well. And the Lord mercifully offers *His* righteousness through salvation in Jesus Christ. With God's help, you can overcome your failings and raise your son to glorify Christ.

Your decision to live in obedience to God will reverberate righteousness in generations to follow. As you increase in your years, how glorious it will be for you to see the godly influence your actions had upon your children and grandchildren. Take it from me, now an empty nester and grandmother of 15: You are giving yourself the most amazing future gift if you guide your children toward loving Christ and loving others with His great love.

Watching our children and grandchildren enjoy one another while visiting our home is the delight of my life. And I know this type of love and unity didn't happen by accident. I grew up in a family characterized by sibling conflict. But because of godly mentors who taught me a better way, my children had an early foundation of learning to love one another with Christ's love. And it is my prayer that this book mentors you to establish a loving foundation as well. For Jesus said, "By this all will know that you are My disciples, if you have love one for another" (John 13:35).

Let it begin with you. As God's love reverberates through you, may His love fill your home with peace and draw your children to know and serve Christ.

THINKING IT THROUGH

With Rebekah's mistakes in mind, list at least three lessons you can learn and apply to your life.

Read Colossians 2:6-7. What four instructions are given to Christians in this passage?

LIVING IT OUT

Confidence in God's sovereignty will help you resist the temptation to manipulate others. How will you work to grow your trust in the character of God?

At the end of your life, what will your children say about your influence? What steps can you take to ensure you are leaving a godly legacy for them?

Watch this chapter's video teaching at
www.rhondastoppe.com/books/moms-raising-sons-to-be-men.

CHAPTER 5

TRAIN HIS BRAIN

Teach Him to Think

Because I said so. How many times have we chanted that mantra? The phrase is sort of a get-out-of-jail-free card for us moms when we don't want to take time to help our children understand the reasons behind our requests. Sometimes "because I said so" is all we have time for. And yes, it's true that children need to be taught to respect their parents' decisions and to obey without needing to engage in the *why* conversation every time they receive instruction from us. Children need to learn to obey their parents so they will also learn to obey God.

But you can't always fall back on "because I said so." If your goal is simply your son's obedience at any cost, and if you never take the time to explain, eventually you will find yourself resorting to anger, frustration, and bribery just to get him to obey—and your son won't grow in understanding. You might achieve temporary compliance, but you will have done nothing to shape his heart.

Instilling obedience in your children is a foundational element of parenting, and your efforts to accomplish this should begin from the very first time your son insists upon rolling over when you are trying to change a messy diaper. And when he is old enough for you to brave the discussion of *why*, you will help him to process, with his mind and heart, the reason behind your instruction. Then his obedience will come from a conscious and heartfelt choice, as opposed to a reflexive response designed to keep you from harping on him or to obtain the trinket with which you are bribing him. If you take advantage of teachable moments when your son is young, he'll be equipped to discern why obedience is best as he matures.

When your son does something wrong, how do you respond? Do you start barking orders? In the moment, it's common for moms to say things like, "Get over here right now. Don't make me come after you." But those types of comments do nothing to train your son's heart. Instead, choose to use the situation as a teachable moment.

Don't just get your son to obey; tell him why. While it is your prerogative as a parent to expect obedience without giving an explanation, it is human nature for a child to genuinely want to know why he is being asked to do or not do something.

The time it takes for you to explain the motivation for obedience may seem like an inconvenience. But the sooner you involve his mind and his heart in this process, the sooner you will equip him to make life decisions on his own—and the sooner you will release yourself from having to monitor his every decision.

Appeal to the Man He Will Become

Developing your son's ability to evaluate his choices will better prepare him to become a man who is able to independently weigh his decisions and choose the right course of action. As your son matures, he will not need you to oversee his every move because you will have instilled in him the ability to determine how to make right choices, and why.

For example, when Brandon was around five years old, his

younger sister, Kayla, would frustrate him by knocking over his LEGO creations. In his anger, Brandon would respond with harsh, hurtful words.

I really did feel for the little guy. Brandon created some amazing structures. His three-year-old sister had no appreciation for all the time and effort he was putting into his projects, or how much he was looking forward to showing his handiwork to Daddy when he came home. Amid these conflicts, I had choices to make:

- I could respond to Kayla with as much anger as Brandon, shouting how wrong she was, while excusing Brandon's harshness as a product of the frustration Kayla had instigated.

- I could ignore the conflict and let them fight with each other.

- I could turn the crisis into a teachable moment.

Kneeling down so my son could look into my eyes, I affirmed his frustration. And I assured him his sister would be corrected for her violation. Then I began to explain to Brandon how kindly God forgives us when we do wrong. I told him God wants us to respond to others the way He treats us. I appealed to the kind and gentle man I knew Brandon wanted to be. I tried to help Brandon see that reacting harshly out of frustration was not good or helpful. And if he began to develop a habit of responding with angry, hurtful words every time his little sister offended him, he would grow into a man who spontaneously reacted to others in the same manner. He would not become a kind man like his daddy.

I further explained to Brandon that I had a responsibility before the Lord to help him grow into a kind, godly man, and that God wanted me to keep him from developing bad habits when he was young, for those habits would be difficult to break when he grew older. (Now, before you get the impression I always responded in a cool, calm, and collected manner to crises around our house, let me set the record straight. For every time I have reacted the way I *knew* I should, there have been multiple times I did not respond properly. But God graciously blessed the times I got it right, and He will bless the times you get it right as well.)

I concluded by telling Brandon, "If I let you talk to Kayla harshly when you are angry, you will one day talk unkindly to your wife and daughters. And I know you want to be a kind man." And, "I know you don't want your sister to marry a man who is harsh or angry. If I allow you to treat her in an unkind manner, she will become accustomed to being treated badly, and may marry a man who is mean because you taught her that's what men do when they are angry."

Yes, those were big concepts and words for a five-year-old, but they weren't too big. I can still see his little face looking into mine, thinking over my words and trying to wrap his mind around what I was teaching him.

When it came to teaching Brandon about his choices over the years, I regularly reminded him of the kind of man God wanted him to become. Even when he was a teenager, I once made him pull the car over so I could remind him that the stress he was under while learning how to drive did not give him permission to speak harshly to his sister in the back seat.

To this day, Brandon will tell you the positive impression my what-kind-of-a-man-do-you-want-to-be speech had upon his development as a man, husband, and father. And thankfully, Kayla chose to marry a very kind man.

What If He's Not a Child?

Psalm 119:9 gives great insight into helping a young man live a pure life: "How can a young man cleanse his way? By taking heed according to Your word."

Kacy was in his twenties when we met him. *Hilarious* is the word I used at first to describe Kacy—one laugh after another. Yet as we came to know of the painful upbringing he had endured, *conflicted* was really a more accurate description.

Kacy had accepted Christ when he was in the eighth grade and living with his abusive, alcoholic father. Although Kacy had professed faith in Christ, he rebelled against God during his teenage years. Early on, Kacy found humor was a way to escape the pain of his home life. Working as a comedian in nightclubs, he found a place where he felt accepted and accomplished.

God developed an instant relationship between our family and Kacy. Week after week he came to our house for Bible study. Gradually the Lord transformed Kacy's thinking through His Word. God's Spirit began to convict Kacy about the life he had chosen to pursue.

We did not have to impose legalism upon Kacy or beat him over the head with our Bibles to get him to see his talent was being wasted upon sinful pleasures. Teaching Kacy from God's Word peeled back the calluses over Kacy's heart, caused him to repent, and stirred within him a desire to serve the Lord. Eventually Kacy resigned from his nightclub work and moved in with our family. The Lord used this season to mature his walk with Christ. His perspectives on life began to be filtered through what he was learning from the Bible. Daily, Kacy discovered how to apply Scripture to his life. This, in turn, cultivated a new passion for God in his heart.

Joyfully, we saw this new foundation in God's truth help Kacy work through painful memories from his childhood. He learned what God's Word said about forgiveness. Over time, Kacy was able to forgive the people who hurt him when he was a child. And soon our student became the teacher. Kacy showed an ability to teach from God's Word, and he joined us in working with the youth at church. He zealously offered to others what had personally transformed his mind, heart, and life.

It soon became apparent that other teens identified with the struggles Kacy had experienced as a young man. His story offered hope to people living in what they thought were hopeless situations.

When Kacy shared the gospel, kids came to Christ. The Lord glorified Himself through the painful childhood Kacy had endured. Experiences that could have destroyed him became instruments to prepare Kacy to serve Christ. By the power of His Word, God molded a man He would use to reach broken and hurting people.

When we first met Kacy, he was the "funny guy" with a troubled past. If we had presented him with a list of behaviors he needed to change, Kacy may very well have complied—for a season. By contrast, waiting for the Lord to inwardly transform Kacy through the power of His Word prepared Kacy to think with the mind of Christ. And over the past two decades we have observed God's transforming work in Kacy as a godly husband and father who did not become a casualty of his abusive upbringing.

The same holds true in parenting. Are you most concerned about getting your son to obey your list of rules? You may be able to coerce, manipulate, and threaten him to follow your standard, but if you have not taught your son from the Bible to think and live in obedience to God, he may one day flounder when he is out from under your watchful eye. Remember, your goal is to guide your son away from dependence upon you toward lifelong dependence upon God.

If your son is older and has not been grounded in the Bible, do not lose heart. Just as God changed Kacy, He is able transform your son's thinking and mold him into a godly man. Here are some steps you may want to consider as you encourage your son toward change:

1. *Keep your focus upon Christ.* Praying for your son and saturating your mind in the Word is vital. The prophet Samuel said, "Far be it from me that I should sin against the Lord in ceasing to pray for you; but I will teach you the good and the right way" (1 Samuel 12:23).

2. *Don't be a hypocrite.* There are no "do-overs" in raising your son. Hypocrisy may be a tool Satan uses to cause

your son to rebel against God. In Mark 7:6-7, Jesus describes hypocrisy: "This people honors Me with their lips, but their heart is far from Me. And in vain they worship Me, teaching as doctrines the commandments of men." Your religious practices will not draw your son to Christ; rather, your genuine love for Christ and for others is what he needs to see.

3. *Make time to interact with your son.* Don't be so busy taking care of tasks you forsake the company of your son. He cannot learn from you if you do not spend time with him.

> **Your goal is to guide your son away from dependence upon you toward lifelong dependence upon God.**

4. *Find a good church youth group.* If you have not been involved in a church, your son may be hesitant to attend a youth group. Pray for the Lord to lead you to a church where *both* you and your son can learn from God's Word. Be sure the church preaches the gospel and is well grounded in the Bible.

Who Am I?

The transformation in Kacy's life did not come because he pulled himself up by his bootstraps and willed himself to change. Instead, he was given a brand-new life defined by what Christ did for him. Kacy inherited an imperishable identity reserved for him in heaven. In the same way, as he learns to apply God's Word to his life, your son can live victoriously, with a new identity in Christ. Those who dwell in Christ are no longer defined by their painful pasts or previous mistakes.

In his book *Instruments in the Redeemer's Hands*, Paul David Tripp states, "We always live out of some kind of identity, and the identities we assign ourselves powerfully influence our responses to life. As people pursue the process of lifelong change, they need to live out of a gospel identity. They, like us, need to be reminded of who they are again and again."[1] Your ultimate goal for your son is that he glorify God through the power of the gospel. A key way to do that is to routinely remind him of his identity in Christ and of the indwelling Spirit who enables him to live in obedience to God. He belongs to Christ, and he is forgiven, adopted, and loved by God. (If your son is not a believer, this is the hope of the gospel you can offer him.)

The concept of identity is very important to grasp as a parent. You may have a child who struggles with anger, shyness, or discouragement. When you describe your son's personality to others, be careful not to label him with negative characteristics. Otherwise, your son may spend the rest of his life wrestling to change the habit of unbiblical thinking about who he is that he learned from you. Worse yet, he may resign himself to living according to the profile you assigned to his character. That's why it's so essential you view him as God sees him, and stress who he is in Christ.

Dr. Tripp goes on to say,

> In the press of everyday life, it is easy to forget who we are. As we try to replace old behaviors with new ones, it is easy to take our eyes off our status as children of God. In fact, the longer we struggle with a problem, the more likely we are to define ourselves by that problem...We come to believe that our problem is who we are. But while these labels may describe particular ways we struggle as sinners in a fallen world, they *are not* our identity! If we allow them to define us, we will live trapped within their boundaries.[2]

And be aware of the ways in which social media influences your son's perception of himself and others. Scrolling through posts of his friends showing their happy lives, excessive purchases, and sexy selfies will make an imprint upon his psyche. And as the Bible says, "As he thinks in his heart, so is he" (Proverbs 23:7).

Be ready to train your son to be cautious and to limit his time online—if or when you allow him to have a social media account. Sit with him as he scrolls, and have conversations with him about what he is viewing so you can show him how to filter it through a biblical perspective. For example, the friends who incessantly post selfies may appear confident to your naïve son. Help him discern how the person may be longing for affirmation or overcompensating for feelings of inferiority.

Let this insight lead him to compassion rather than judgment. Helping your son develop a heart of tenderness toward his peers is a wonderful way you can help him develop into a kind, caring man who looks beyond a person's surface to discern their genuine need— the need to know one's worth through the love of Christ.

The Mommy Club

The Lord used my friend Molly to teach me the concept of identifying my children in positive ways with my words. My husband and I deliberately became friends with Molly and her husband, Vaughn, because we loved their kids. They had three elementary-aged children who were simply a delight. We enjoyed them so much we even went on a weeklong vacation with their family back when we had no children of our own.

Molly made an impression upon me when she responded to her children's accomplishments by saying things like, "You're so smart!" After my first child, Meredith, was born, I recall Molly reading a book to her. Each time Meredith pointed to the picture when Molly asked her to, she would respond, "You're so smart!"

Molly explained to me the importance of telling my daughter she was intelligent. She also warned, "Never tell your child she is stupid or dumb when she makes a mistake. She will believe you and will live according to those expectations." Molly does not have a

PhD in child development, but she clearly understands how words can influence children's perceptions of themselves.

The Bible instructs older women to teach the younger women to "love their children" (Titus 2:4). We can be fairly certain that Timothy's mother, Eunice, was mentored by her godly mother, Lois. Follow Eunice's example and seek out a godly, older woman who properly loves her children and God's Word. Become a friend to this woman. Join the Bible study she attends. Ask her over for coffee. Invite her to speak truth into your life. (And then don't be offended when she does.) Do not assign her the burden of pursuing you; you make the time to meet with her. Study the way she interacts with her children and learn from her example. The effective teacher is one who makes time to continually learn. As Dr. Howard Hendricks wisely said, "If you stop growing today, you stop teaching tomorrow."[3]

God chose Eunice to prepare Timothy, and He has chosen you to teach your son. Study the Bible, read parenting books with a biblical foundation, pray, and pursue relationships with godly mothers who have walked the road before you. In these ways you will prepare yourself to be the mother you have always hoped you would be. And you will also prepare your son for a lifetime of being used by God for special purposes He has already planned in the future.

THINKING IT THROUGH

How can your son find his identity in Christ? How might this practice help him grow to be a godly man?

According to Romans 12:2, what specifically helps to transform a person? What part does Scripture play in training you and your son to discern God's will?

LIVING IT OUT

Your goal should never be to motivate your son to simply do good deeds, but to teach him how to become like Christ. What are some specific steps you can take to help your son develop Christlike character qualities?

Watch this chapter's video teaching at
www.rhondastoppe.com/books/moms-raising-sons-to-be-men

PART TWO

GUIDING YOUR SON TOWARD GODLY MANHOOD

CHAPTER 6

PARENTING WITHOUT REGRETS

The Discipline of a Disciple

Don't touch that! I'm not buying candy for you. I'm not kidding, don't make me count! One…two…don't make me get to three. You seriously don't want me to get to three!" cried the mother of the two-year-old in the checkout line, her voice rising higher with each threat.

Does this scenario sound familiar? We have all heard *that* mother. And maybe you have also *been* that mother. Have you found yourself embarrassed by the judgmental stares of onlookers as you coaxed or, through clenched teeth, pleaded with your child to comply? Then to prevent further public humiliation, have you given in to your toddler's demands?

Before I was a mother, I arrogantly passed judgment upon moms who seemed unable to control their children. I remember thinking, *If I were that child's mother, I wouldn't allow such disobedient behavior.* Fantasizing about what kind of mother I would be, I imagined how I would calmly make a request, and my children would respectfully comply.

But it had never occurred to me *how* I would teach my children to respect me. I just assumed I would figure out my parenting skills as I went along. After I had my first child, I became humbly aware of how unprepared I was to be a mother. Intimidated by this new role of motherhood, I asked the Lord to send a godly mentor who could help guide me through this daunting responsibility.

Shortly after I prayed about this, the Lord brought my friend Molly and her husband, Vaughn, into our lives. One afternoon Vaughn and Molly, along with their three young children, joined us for lunch at my in-laws' house. While my husband visited with Vaughn, his four-year-old son, Adam, reached up to touch a valuable figurine that was displayed on a shelf.

Discerning Adam's intent, Vaughn calmly said, "Adam, please don't touch that." Then, without skipping a beat, Vaughn resumed talking with my husband.

Adam carefully pulled his hand back and stood looking at the figurine without touching it. Steve and I were in awe. Vaughn had not raised his voice. He had not hovered over his son to make sure he would not touch the figurine. He fully expected Adam to respond in obedience. And Adam did!

Steve said, "How'd you do that? How'd you get him to obey like that? Without raising your voice, or making any threats?"

Vaughn responded, "We trained him not to touch things without permission." That day, we asked Vaughn and Molly to mentor us as parents.

As Steve and I spent time with our mentors, what intrigued us most was how much they delighted in their children. Everyone in their family genuinely loved and enjoyed each other's company. Vaughn and Molly had somehow instilled within their kids a loving respect for their parents, their siblings, and for God. Their godly example established our trust in their parental instruction.

Key Principles for Godly Parenting

Through Bible study, and through the examples of godly women,

I learned many parenting principles that helped me raise my children in a God-honoring way. In this part of the book, each chapter will examine one key principle for effective parenting. Although these seven principles do not comprise an exhaustive list of principles for training your children, they will give you the most foundational elements of raising up your son to be a godly man.

PRINCIPLE 1: Teaching Your Son to Respect Authority Prepares Him to Respect God's Authority

———

The Lord has set up an order of authority within the home, with promised blessings to those who obey. "Children, obey your parents in the Lord, for this is right. 'Honor your father and mother,' which is the first commandment with promise: 'that it may be well with you and you may live long on the earth'" (Ephesians 6:1-3).

Teaching your son to submit to your God-given authority over him will establish within him a foundation for respecting the Lord. God has assigned to you the responsibility for raising your son according to the Bible's guidelines, so don't apologize for imposing your authority upon him. Truly, if you do not provide godly guidance for your son, you allow him to disobey the Lord's mandate. Without exception, God does *not* bless disobedience.

If you forfeit your position of leadership by allowing your son to independently determine his choices, you will inadvertently teach him that he is free to do whatever he wants. Without careful direction from you, your son may develop a self-governing attitude, believing he answers to no one. In their book *Instructing a Child's Heart*, Tedd and Margy Tripp address the impact self-government has upon a child:

> By the age that they are ready for school, most children see themselves as autonomous decision-makers.

> Parents give away their authority in thousands of different transactions…[The] child is not learning that God, who is good, has given him parents whom he is to obey; and it is a blessing to live under God's authority. He is rather being taught to reject any authority other than himself…Freedom is not being able to do whatever you want; freedom is knowing and loving God and living joyfully under the authority structures that He has ordained.[1]

Your son may develop a distorted view of freedom if you allow him to govern himself. You should help him mature into a man who will eventually be independent from *your* authority, but *never* independent from God's authority. As you train your son to honor your God-given position of leadership, you will help mold him into a man who respects the Lord's authority.

Where do young adults learn resentment against authority? At a young age, they develop a distorted view of freedom by governing themselves. We don't have to look far to see the effects of a generation characterized by entitlement and rebellion. And what's a mother to do? How can we affect the culture in which our sons are being raised? What can we do to change the trajectory of a rebellious generation?

We can stay true to our callings. Throughout countless generations the Lord has used the powerful vocation of motherhood to equip His servants. God promises to take your little and make much of your work.

Here are a few important practices:

Saturate his mind with Scripture. Read the Bible to your child and train him to memorize Scripture. This equips him with the sword of God's Word. The Word of God, hidden in his heart, can draw him away from temptation and guide his path toward Christ.

Saturate his mind with Christian music. Music is a powerful influence over your son's worldview. Satan, who was the musician of heaven before his fall, also understands how music can shape your son's developing mind. The devil will attempt to use ungodly music to drown out the biblical values you have been teaching your son. In our decades of youth ministry, many times a mother would come to my husband with concerns over her son's rebellious attitude. Because Steve had learned through experience the impact negative music had upon teens, his first question was always, "What type of music is he listening to?"

Christian music, on the other hand, can lay a biblical foundation in your son's thoughts. When our kids were young, we put them to bed each night listening to Steve Green's *Hide 'Em in Your Heart* songs. Because each song was word-for-word Scripture, our children memorized a great number of Bible verses that have stayed with them throughout life. Even now, more than 20 years later, our children can still sing the Scripture passages they memorized as they drifted off to dreamland.

> If you forfeit your position of leadership by allowing your son to independently determine his choices, you will inadvertently teach him that he is free to do whatever he wants.

When our granddaughter Karis was two years old, she came to our ranch for a visit. When our peacocks' screeching frightened her (yes, we have over a dozen peacocks on our ranch), she immediately started singing, "When I am afraid I will trust in you." Steve and I smiled, because another generation was learning how to apply biblical knowledge to the situations of life.

Saturate his generation with prayer. God is searching for people who will stand in the gap with intercession for this generation. In Ezekiel 22:30, God says, "I sought for a man among them who would make a wall, and stand in the gap before Me on behalf of the land, that I should not destroy it; but I found no one." May it never be said of this generation that the Lord could not find us as mothers on our knees, interceding before the Lord upon their behalf.

The Laboratory of Learning

God intends our homes to be the training ground for life. Think of your house as a laboratory in which you practice the values you teach your son. Your instruction should be deliberate and on-going. You want to have times when you set aside your other tasks and focus on teaching your son how to conduct himself. Don't limit your training to simply reacting to his behavior—that puts him in the driver's seat, so to speak. You need to take the lead so he understands how the parent-child relationship works.

Remember, your son is not a distraction to your ministry—he *is* your ministry. Amid the pressures of life, it is easy to forget that your focus should be on molding his character to glorify God. Begin each morning by asking God to remind you to maintain your proper priorities throughout the day.

The best place to nurture the character quality of self-control is in the privacy of your own home. Don't make the mistake of setting up a living environment in your home that is so babyproof that your son never has an opportunity to learn to restrain himself.

Likewise, don't wait until you are visiting someone else's house to teach your son temperance. Having other people watch you correct him will likely create stress and may lead to angry frustration on your part, or to pandering to your son's whims. Either response makes *everyone* uncomfortable. (And don't be surprised if your next invitation to visit is a meeting at a fast-food restaurant with a playground.)

Vaughn and Molly emphasized that we needed to begin early when we trained our children to learn self-control. So when Meredith, our first child, was not yet one year old, I set aside some time to teach her not to touch fragile items. In our formal living room, I purposefully placed some glass trinkets on the coffee table. I then laid my daughter's blanket on the floor and scattered some of her favorite toys on the blanket. When I set Meredith down to play, I told her I was going to read a magazine, and she could play with her toys.

I sat on the sofa and looked intently at the magazine. Not long after we settled into our activities, my daughter began to look around the room. Landing her gaze upon the glass objects on the table, she scooted over and pulled herself up to get a better look.

I intentionally stopped reading and made eye contact with my toddler. In a calm and quiet voice I clearly defined the rule: "You are not allowed to touch these because they will break."

With the goal of ensuring Meredith comprehended what I was saying, I moved down to her level, looked her in the eyes, and said in a gentle tone of voice, "Remember, I said you're not allowed to touch. These are Mommy's pretty treasures. Do you understand? Don't touch."

Back to the couch I went, acting completely distracted by my magazine. Meredith looked at me and then scooted over to the coffee table again. I watched out of the corner of my eye as she studied me, and then one of the glass treasures. Then with her eyes on me, she reached out to touch the forbidden fruit. She instinctively knew to sneak her hand upward while I was distracted!

As Meredith reached for the trinket, she kept her eyes on me to see how I would respond. In a normal tone of voice, I calmly said, "No-no. Not allowed to touch. Remember? You will break it." I moved my daughter back to her blanket to play with her toys.

And guess what? Soon, Meredith was on her way back over to touch what she had clearly understood was a no-no. Meredith and I spent the better part of the day going through all this. Because I had scheduled this time for training, I could see the lesson through to the end. I was able to maintain a clear objective and respond in a calm and loving manner without losing my temper. By the time my daughter went down for her afternoon nap, Mommy was victorious...and needed a nap as well.

Through many "don't touch workshops," each of my children learned they could not wear me down or win over in defiance. However, because children are genuinely curious about how various objects feel, I eventually implemented a *one-finger touch* rule. Each child quickly learned the self-restraint to touch gently, with their pointer finger, without picking up or breaking fragile objects. This enabled them to satisfy their curiosity and still understand the importance of obedience and respecting parental authority.

Looking back, every minute I spent training my children while they were young paid off in great dividends of respect when they became teenagers. Any sacrifice you make now to discipline your son will establish a regard for your authority that will transfer over into his teen years. When your son reaches adolescence, his respect for you will be strongly influenced by what has been established early in his life. Any matters not settled during your son's "terrible twos" will likely surface in full force when he is in middle school.

The terrible twos and adolescence are very similar. Their emotions are very intense, and you must choose your battles. I often tell mothers, "The biggest difference between your toddler and your tween is one has diaper rash and the other has acne." The best time to neutralize conflicts with your adolescent son is a decade earlier!

Talk *to* Him, Not *at* Him

As you train your son, make clear communication a priority. By paying close attention to him while you are speaking, you eliminate any possibility of confusion and learn to discern whether he actually comprehends your instructions.

Maybe you have developed a habit of talking *at* your son rather than *to* him. For example, while you're cooking dinner or working on the computer, you've found yourself barking orders over your shoulder, like, "Stop doing that. You know I don't like it when you do that. You're making me mad." Such communication does not qualify as giving him instruction. This is nothing more than *responding* to behavior rather than *shaping* it.

If you end up raising your voice to get your son to respond, he will learn to ignore your commands until you reach what he comes to know as your breaking point. When that happens, he is in control, not you. And if you attempt to instill obedience while you are trying to focus on other things, you are more likely to throw out empty commands until you lose your temper—or just as damaging, until you ignore your son's wrong behavior altogether. That's why it is so essential to set aside times for training. That way, you can give your son your full attention, and you can stay calm and reason with him in a loving yet firm manner.

Whatever your son's age, you should establish a pattern of taking time to communicate clearly and calmly what behaviors are not acceptable, and why. Now, telling him *why* does not undermine your authority. Rather, it teaches him to think through your command, and allows him to realize there is a consequence if he chooses to disobey.

As you speak to your son, make a habit of looking into his eyes. This will enable you to assess his interpretation of your instruction. To most effectively parent your son, take the time to see what *he* sees, hear what *he* hears, and think what *he* thinks. Know your son well so you can discern what is going on in his mind as he processes your directions.

When you give instructions to your son, ask him to repeat back to you what he heard you say. This will give you the assurance he clearly understands your request. If he does not, and you discipline him for defiance, you will confuse and frustrate him.

We're in This Together

Godly discipline should not be viewed as a competition for power. Help your son understand the roles God has assigned each of you in the parent-child relationship. Instill in him the idea that God has given you 18 years, or while he is living in your home, to teach him how to obey God and say no to sinful desires. And let your son know that his role is to learn how to follow the Lord and resist temptation so he is prepared to stand strong when he is a grown man.

What about the times when your son disobeys you and breaks the rules? Don't be surprised. Everyone sins, and your son needs to know what to do when that happens. When he does wrong, use his offense as an opportunity to teach him how to make things right in his relationship with the Lord and with you, or whomever he has sinned against.

Work to build a relationship of trust with your son. Empathize with him as he battles with temptation. Telling your son that you identify with his struggle because you wrestle with sin as well will help him believe you really do understand his trials. When you make yourself vulnerable in this way, he will likely come to seek your counsel.

If you try to *seem* as though you are never tempted, your pretense could serve to alienate your son from you. He may think you cannot relate to his struggles and therefore couldn't possibly know how to help him. Or worse, he will see through your hypocrisy and be turned off by Christianity altogether. By living an honest, transparent life in front of your son, you can teach him how to know victory over temptation and sin. While it is not wise to tell him about every sinful desire with which you struggle, you *can* help your son realize how closely *you* must walk with the Lord to live an obedient life.

Here are some practical ways to live with sincerity before your son:

- When you lose your temper, ask your son to forgive you. You could say something like, "Ephesians 4:32 says we are to be kind to one another. Please forgive me for speaking harshly to you. I have asked God to forgive me for disobeying His Word and to help me respond to you with kindness."

- If you have gossiped in your son's presence, tell him the Lord has convicted you about your sin. Say you have asked for God to forgive you and help you to keep your tongue from evil (1 Peter 3:10). Ask your son to forgive you as well.

- When your son has wronged you, forgive him. Explain how God gives you the ability to forgive and not hold a grudge.

Did you notice how many times the word *forgive* was used in the above list? Forgiveness should be a characteristic of God's people. By asking for your son's forgiveness, you'll demonstrate how all of us are equal before God's righteous judgment, and how all of us are desperately in need of God's grace.

I know a young man named Nathan who works for a Christian camp. He is a wonderful servant, joyful, and passionate about his ministry. Having never met Nathan's mother, I was curious about her influence upon his development as a godly man. I asked him, "In one word, describe your mother for me." He did not even hesitate before he smiled and responded, "*Forgiving*. She is the most forgiving person I have ever known."

Wouldn't your heart be blessed beyond measure if your son made that statement about you? Follow God's example and let your home be a place where forgiveness is readily given and received.

The Lord Is My Banner

As your son learns how to live the victorious Christian life, he needs to believe you are in his corner, praying he will be strong in the face of temptation. When your son struggles with sin, remind him of the story in which Joshua fought against the enemy while Moses held up the rod of God (Exodus 17:8-16). As long as Moses kept his arms reached toward heaven, Joshua had the strength he needed for victory.

From this example, you can learn some specific ways to encourage your son when he struggles against temptation:

Paint a word picture for your son. Help him imagine you on the hill, praying for his victory, while he, like Joshua, fights as a valiant warrior of God (Ephesians 6:12-13). Teach your son that the

Lord made Joshua victorious because he was faithful and because of Moses's prayer, and you are confident God can do the same for him.

Celebrate the victory of Joshua. Tell your son you celebrate his courageous triumphs as well. You can always rejoice together in the tangible ways God comes to the defense and help of His beloved children.

Pour courage into your son by telling him the Lord is his banner. On days when your son is obviously struggling with a sinful behavior, pray together, asking God to help him *make right choices today*. Remind your son that the same God who helped Joshua will help him. This will help your son to realize God sees his struggle and desires to offer him strength for victory.

The best teachable moments come in times of disobedience. Your goal is not perfection. You're not trying to raise a perfect adult, but one who knows how to repent and make things right in his relationship with Christ—and with others. Romans 2:4 says that it is God's kindness that leads us toward repentance. So follow the Lord's example and kindly lead your son to God's grace by teaching him how to turn away from his sin and seek God's forgiveness. And pray for the Lord to draw his heart quickly toward repentance whenever he sins.

Promise your son you will faithfully serve as his prayer warrior. One of the most powerful influences you can have upon your son's development into a godly man is to pray diligently on his behalf, just as Moses did for Joshua. Your position as intercessor will prepare your son to be a man who relies upon his God for strength, and not upon his mother. Commit yourself to praying for your son daily as he fights against temptation. Some common temptations your son may face are lying, being unkind to his friends, taking vengeance on someone, viewing pornography, or cheating on his schoolwork. Throughout the day, pray for your son to resist these and other struggles.

Imagine the courage Joshua would have drawn from looking

up to the hill and seeing Moses's arms raised toward heaven on his behalf. You can infuse the same kind of courage into your son by letting him know you pray regularly for him. As an adult, my son Brandon says he still finds it a great source of strength to know his momma is at home praying for him while he is out slaying dragons. I often send him a text, "I'm praying for you," to which he simply responds, "Thanks, Momma."

Find ways to encourage your son. Perhaps you could put a note in his lunch box that reminds him you are praying for him. Or, instead of a note, you could write a small, secret symbol on his lunch napkin to remind him of your intercessions for him. (Consider an encrypted message understood only by the two of you so his friends won't get nosy and tease him.)

When my son was attending public school, each morning I encouraged him by praying for God to make him victorious over the day's temptations. I would pray, *Lord, lead him not into temptation, and deliver him from the evil one today* (Matthew 6:13). I can think of no better way to pray for your son than to pray along the same lines that Jesus Himself taught us to pray.

The Work of a Disciple

The effective, godly discipline of your son will require that you discipline yourself first. To train your son well, you must commit to laying aside distractions in your own life that will steal away the precious time you need to build a foundation in your son's heart.

When you take the time to teach your son self-control and respectful obedience, you give him a truly wonderful gift. Not only will people likely be drawn to his well-mannered, obedient demeanor, but more importantly, you will cultivate within your son a heart prepared to submit to God's authority. And all the sacrifices you make on his behalf will be repaid abundantly as you see your son grow into a man who has the wisdom to make wise choices and pursue godliness in his life.

THINKING IT THROUGH

Read Titus 2:3-5 and write a list of the qualities of a godly older woman. Which of these qualities stand out to you most, and why?

LIVING IT OUT

Will you ask God to direct you to an older woman who can mentor you as a mother? Looking again at Titus 2:3-5, what would you find most helpful to learn from a godly older woman, and why?

Watch this chapter's video teaching at
www.rhondastoppe.com/books/moms-raising-sons-to-be-men.

CHAPTER 7

IMPART THE VISION

The Man He Will Become

What do you imagine when you ponder your son's future? Is he smart, talented, funny, athletic? What can you do to help your son develop the skills that best prepare him for life? How can you help him be the kind of man who honors God with his talents?

Your job as a mother is not to guess what your son's abilities are and then coerce him into following a specific path in life. The Lord already knows your son's strengths. After all, He gave those abilities and gifts to your son. God is the One who can establish His intentions for your son. You have the responsibility to yield and work alongside God in preparing your son for a future that honors Christ.

As a mother, you are to adopt godly aspirations for your son as you walk in close fellowship with the Lord. The Bible says, "Delight yourself also in the LORD, and He shall give you the desires of your heart" (Psalm 37:4). To discern God's desires for your son, learn to daily take pleasure in who God is through prayer, worship, and Bible study. In so doing, the Holy Spirit will help you to renounce your personal agendas and instead seek the Lord's plans for you and your son.

In her book *Women on the Edge*, Cindi McMenamin says, "We often quote Psalm 37:4 as our 'guarantee' that God is going to come through with granting our desires...[But] I believe God is saying, 'Delight yourself in Me, and I will you give you desires for what I desire, and then I'll gladly grant them.'"[1]

God cares so much about your son's future that He will place longings within him and then accomplish those desires through him. Are you willing to leave your son's future in God's hands? In Psalm 138:8, King David said with confidence, "The LORD will perfect that which concerns me." In Psalm 144:3, David spoke in awe of God's involvement in his life: "LORD, what is man, that You take knowledge of him? Or the son of man, that You are mindful of him?"

God is very much involved in our children's lives. We don't need to get in the way. There are days I simply laugh out loud when I ponder how much the Lord has been engaged in my children's everyday lives. As each child has chosen to walk in obedience to the Lord, God faithfully "perfects that which concerns" them. Yes, God is mindful of your son's future. As a mother, you can rest safely in God's sovereignty. He is able to complete the work He has begun in your son!

The Result of One Mother's Faith

Susanna Wesley was the mother of the great John Wesley. History records her as a woman whose faith was genuine. Her faithful example had a profound influence upon her children and the generations to follow.

Susanna's son John grew up to be a famous evangelist. For more than 50 years during the eighteenth century, he tirelessly preached the gospel all over England and the American colonies. Wesley delivered some thousand messages annually as he made his way through the country on horseback, traveling about 8,000 miles each year. Wesley was described by his contemporaries as "a man on fire for God, looking out upon the world as his parish, studying as he rode, preaching in season and out of season...He is always at it."[2]

Much more could be said about the amazing influence John Wesley had upon his generation. But what do we know about his mother, Susanna? When she looked into the face of her little boy, did she know she was raising a man whom God would use to evangelize England and America? How could she? Susanna was a mother, just like you and me. And just as God called Susanna to live in a manner that would draw her children to Christ and teach them to know and love Him, He calls us today to do the same.

Proverbs 10:9 promises, "He who walks with integrity walks securely." The original Hebrew word for *integrity* had the sense of "living what you believe."[3] Susanna Wesley's godly example influenced her son because she was faithful to live with integrity, to reflect God's character in her everyday life. Her genuine love for the Lord and her dedicated service to her family undoubtedly captured her son's affections.

If you want to win your son's heart and respect for God, then pursue Christ with all sincerity, as Susanna did. As you allow God to transform you into the image of His Son, He can use your example to prepare your son to reflect Christ as well. If your son believes your faith is genuine, his respect for you will grow, and he will trust you to help him discover his God-given desires and gifts.

As you obey God on a daily basis, He can also do great things through you—and your son. God is able to prepare your son through you or in spite of you. The choice is yours. Will you ask the Lord to help you lead your son by example?

In chapter 6, I introduced you to the first of seven principles for effective parenting. Now let's look at the second one:

PRINCIPLE 2: Have a Clear Idea of the Kind of Man God Calls Your Son to Be

———

"I don't care if you are a lawyer or a ditch digger, as long as you do your work for God's glory." My husband, Steve, has said that many times—to his youth group, to our children, and to our sons-in-law.

Steve's point is this: True success is found in living for the Lord. You see, you can raise your son to be the most educated, accomplished *whatever*. But if he misses the purpose for his life—to reflect the image of God—he will never be truly content, and more importantly, God will not be glorified in his life.

Should your son grow up to find his worth in anything other than his relationship with Christ, he will miss what he was created to do—glorify God and enjoy Him forever. Success is not to be measured in terms of one's occupation or achievements, but in living for the glory of God (1 John 2:15-16; 4:4-6). As 1 Corinthians 10:31 says, "Whatever you do, do all to the glory of God." By your own example, then, teach your son to aim to do *all* things, even the basic and mundane, for God's glory.

A Proper Perspective of Work

Teaching your son the difference between laboring for God's glory and idolizing his career for his own prestige is no easy task. Kept in proper perspective, work is a good thing. The Lord made men to enjoy occupying themselves with a vocation.

The Bible teaches men are required to work so they can provide for their families (2 Thessalonians 3:10-12). Now, many people view work negatively and assume it is a consequence of Adam and Eve's fall into sin. But in Genesis 2:15, we read that God assigned Adam the job of tending the garden of Eden *before* there was sin in the world. So we know work is good because, when God finished making all of creation, He saw all He had made and said it was good (Genesis 1:31).

If you teach your son a proper perspective of work, it will serve as the foundation of his work ethic throughout his adult life. The book of Proverbs is a wonderful place to turn to for principles that will help instill a God-honoring attitude toward work.

My husband has always been a hard worker. I know how much he enjoys seeing his finished accomplishments after a day of labor. But I never really understood how deeply men gained satisfaction from doing a good day's work until our son Brandon was about 12 years old.

We live on a ranch in Northern California. There are always chores to be done, and when Brandon was in middle school, I would try to get him to help out with the necessary tasks.

However, it was during this same time that Brandon was working through his—how shall I say this nicely?—*moody years* of adolescence. So there were days when Steve came home from work to find me in tears. Usually the conflicts my son and I had were over things of little significance. But as an adolescent attempting to become a man, Brandon felt disrespected when his momma told him what to do. (At the time, I was heartbroken that my boy was clearly pulling away from me.) I see now how I misunderstood Brandon's pulling away to be an act of rebellion. I later learned it was a young man's normal longing for respect that plays out in this manner. In his book *Mother and Son*, Dr. Emerson Eggerichs explains:

> When a mother and son get into a conflict—a very stressful event to both—the son feels far more disrespected than he feels unloved, and he craves respect more than love. But how many mothers detect this, and if they do, how many know what to say or do? Who has coached a mom to ask, "Is what I am about to say going to sound respectful or disrespectful to my son?"... The good news

is that once mom sees this need in her boy, she can use this information with prudence. She need only say, "I am not trying to show you disrespect when I confront your misbehavior." Just using the word *disrespect* eases his stress.[4]

One evening when Steve arrived home, he decided he'd had enough of my tears and Brandon's attitude. I cringed as Steve called Brandon to come downstairs. There was a part of me that wanted Steve to intervene and be my knight in shining armor. But there was another part of me that wanted to protect my little boy from the strong correction I knew he would incur from his father, even though I knew Brandon deserved a good reprimand.

Steve didn't waste time getting to the point: "Boy, I will not come home to my wife in tears because you won't do what you're told."

I was thinking, *Okay, I'm liking where this is going so far.*

Steve went on: "This is my wife, and I will not allow anyone to disrespect her. Do you understand?"

Brandon nodded.

"From now on, you don't have to answer to your mom for any of the chores around the house." Brandon put out his chest and almost smiled with relief at the prospect of not having to be under my "unreasonable rule." But then Steve said, "But boy, now you answer to me, and I am not as easy to work for. I also won't accept excuses. Tomorrow I want you to take a pick and shovel and begin digging a ditch from the house to the shed. I want it deep because I am going to run electrical wires through the ditch."

Steve paused for a moment, then concluded, "You get up first thing tomorrow, and you get to work. And I don't want your mother to remind you. In fact, she is not involved in this at all. You work for me. Got it?"

Again, Brandon nodded.

The next morning, before Steve left for work, he reminded me, "You are not to be involved. If he does not do the work, *I* will deal with it when I get home. Don't remind him. Don't even address it."

When Brandon came downstairs, he was dressed in work clothes. He quietly ate his breakfast, then went outside to begin working. He worked for most of the day.

Upon coming back into the house, I expected Brandon to complain about how hard the ground was and how difficult the labor had been. I thought he might even blame me for selling him out to his father, thus incurring the hard labor. But to my surprise, Brandon had a huge smile on his face. He said, "Wow, I got a lot done. Come see how far I have dug!" Brandon's sisters and I went out to look, and we celebrated the wonderful job he had done.

When Steve came home, Brandon was much cooler about his accomplishment. He waited until his father asked him if he had worked on the ditch, then offered to take his dad outside to let him see how far he had gotten. The two men went outside. From in the house I could hear Steve's words of encouragement for a job well done. Then, to my surprise, Brandon said, "Just wait until tomorrow. I will get even farther!"

Brandon's response to all this hard work surprised me. I had fully expected him to grow frustrated, even angry, with each swing of the pick into the hard ground. After all, his assignment had come in the form of discipline. Instead, each evening, he came into the house tired and satisfied, eager to show his father his progress.

This response gave me a glimpse into how God has created men to find a sense of accomplishment in a good day's work. And how boys long to be respected as men. It was also apparent how important a father's affirmation is to a son. (If you're a single mom, don't fret. I know countless hardworking men who were raised by a single mother without a father's validation. In the single mom chapter, we will talk more about how single moms can enlist godly men to affirm their sons.)

You should have seen how excited Brandon was when he took Steve out to survey the finished project. He could hardly wait for the next morning, when Steve would show him how to run the conduit through the ditch and teach him how to pull the wire that would bring power to the shed. On the day the lights were turned on in the shed, by the whoops and hollers coming from the yard, you would have thought Steve and Brandon were lighting a great palace!

Because God created men to derive satisfaction from a job well done, your son should be assigned age-appropriate tasks that allow him to cultivate a sense of accomplishment and responsibility. When your son reaches adolescence, if possible allow his father or another man he respects to be the one he answers to in the work arena. Surrendering the authority over your son's chores to his dad provides a way for your son to learn his work ethic from a male role model.

Hard Work Works

If you do not live on a ranch with many chores to be done, you have other options! Denel, a dear friend of mine, took to heart Brandon's ditch-digging story when her son, Tyler, was an adolescent.

Denel and Tyler lived in a town with finely manicured yards. So Denel made mowing the lawn Tyler's work. He found such gratification in the assignment that he grew skilled at mowing in neat diagonal rows with great accuracy. Whenever Tyler became frustrated with his schoolwork, Denel modified the ditch-digging idea and sent Tyler on a 30-minute bike ride. She was amazed how different his attitude was after he spent time exercising. And this helped Tyler to set goals for himself. Every time he rode his bike, he tried to go a greater distance than before during his allotted 30 minutes.

Tyler learned to enjoy hard work. He is now a young adult who is employed as a big equipment operator. His boss hired him right out of high school because of his well-established work ethic.

When your son does well, honor his efforts. Patting him on the back for a job well done is important. I have heard mothers say they do not want to encourage their son to be prideful, so they play down their son's accomplishments. Better think twice about that approach, Mom. Your words hold a great deal of weight. Your words of affirmation and inspiration will give your son confidence to attempt new endeavors. And as you acknowledge that your son's hard work is pleasing to the Lord, teach him to give God the glory for the abilities he has.

When Brandon was in kindergarten, he participated in his first "performance" in a school Christmas program. I made sure to sit in the front row to help my shy little boy find the courage to sing his part in the play. When he finished a particularly difficult song, Brandon looked into the audience, found my face, and winked at his momma, who was applauding wildly.

You can imagine how my heart melted at his precious gesture. Over the years, I have had many additional opportunities to sit in the audience while my son performs. Whenever I am able to attend, I make sure to find a place in the front row. Even as an adult, there are times when Brandon has looked out from the stage, made eye contact with me, and winked. Each time, I think back to the little five-year-old in his red cardigan sweater, nervously singing in the school Christmas program.

When your son is facing challenging opportunities, your godly affirmation may be exactly what he needs to summon the courage and strength to do well. If you withhold encouraging comments or nitpick at your son's work because he did not meet up to your possibly unrealistic standard, you may end up doing more harm than good.

> When your son is facing challenging opportunities, your godly affirmation may be exactly what he needs to summon the courage and strength to do well.

Teaching your son how to take pride in his work without becoming prideful requires careful balance. When you talk to your son about work, teach him to think biblically. As you help him discern his strengths, remind him to thank God for his abilities. Encouraging him to be grateful will train your son to recognize his skills are a gift from God. That will help discourage any arrogance over his personal successes.

As you help your son consider his work options for the future, do so with his abilities in mind. Help him to take advantage of what he is good at. Rather than focus on the notoriety or money to be made from certain careers, help your son assess his skills and guide him in a direction that will prepare him to support a family and to serve the Lord.

Ambassador for Christ

The Bible teaches that believers are citizens of the kingdom of heaven. We are passing through this life on our way to eternity. And as we do so, God wants us to represent Him to others, to those who are not believers.

Daily, your son is observing what you say and how you live. And the Lord has uniquely placed you in your son's life to joyfully reflect Christ's character to him. You must *deliberately* live each day in a manner that causes your son to *want* to know Jesus.

Does that sound intimidating? Please don't shrink back thinking you'll never be able to measure up to this type of ambassador living. I am right there with you. Without God's daily help I would have lost sight of my purpose to live as an ambassador for Christ. Believe me, there were many days amid the hard work of raising a family that I was just trying to keep my head above water and not lose my temper. But, Momma, don't lose hope. Live one day at a time. On the days you live in a way that might draw your son toward Christ, thank God for His help. And on the days you don't, thank God for His forgiveness. Even on your hard days, God can be glorified as your children observe your frailty and your need to rely on His strength amid the pressures of life.

You will have ups and downs—guaranteed. Don't beat yourself up on those long days of survival. Every moment of every day can reflect Christ's glory when your kids see you regularly going back to the throne of grace for help. This is the normal Christian life. And living in transparent reliance upon God is what your kids need to see, so that they too will know how to rely upon His strength rather than their own.

As God's ambassador, you have been called to the most extraordinary responsibility a person could have. There is no higher calling than to know and represent God Almighty to your generation, and especially to your son. Your genuine joy in living the Christian life will likely stir within your son an appetite for the Lord. (Adversely, if you settle for mediocre existence, your apathy may repel your son.)

In his book *Teaching to Change Lives*, Dr. Howard Hendricks says,

> Most of us settle for communicating the message with the intellectual component only. We rely too heavily on words alone...The most effective communication always includes an *emotional* ingredient—the *feeling* factor, the *excitement* element. If I claim to be committed to the eternal truth of the Word of God, then it must be reflected in my values, in what I prize, in where I put my time and my money, in what I get excited about... We're teaching the most exciting truth in the world—eternal truth—and doing it as if it were cold mashed potatoes.[5]

When your son can see you living a holy life, walking in a God-honoring way, and enjoying the presence of the Lord, you will earn the privilege of being a living testimony to him. And he is a lot more likely to listen to what you have to say.

What's Love Got to Do with It?

God wants you to live in such a way His divine nature defines you and draws others to salvation. Jesus said the priority of life is to love God with all of your being. And then you'll be able to love others, with His love—beginning with your own children (Mark 12:30-31). For this to happen, you need to deliberately pursue intimacy with God through prayer, Bible study, and fellowship with other believers who deeply love God.

These days fellowship can mean anything from a coffee date with friends to a virtual Bible study. Social media is a form of fellowship too. Even though some of the podcasters and influencers you might follow have no idea who you are, be aware as you follow their posts and listen to their messages that you are being influenced by their worldview. So ask God to help you discern with whom you should "fellowship." Look for friends, both in person or online, who share Scripture and uplifting, Christ-honoring content. And while you're at it, become a friend who faithfully speaks in a manner that reflects your love for Christ.

Jesus said the world will be able to distinguish His disciples by how they love one another (John 13:34-35). As you walk in the Spirit—that is, you yield to His leading—God's love will shine through you to others. Your sincere affection for your son and others will testify of your genuine faith to a watching world. Those who emanate Christ's loving character shine like stars, pointing others to the way of salvation. Your genuine love for the Lord can draw your son to Christ and put you in the position to teach him God's vision for the man that God desires him to become.

As a mother, you are a very influential person in your son's life. If you train his heart right, you can inspire him to attempt great feats and to honor God with his accomplishments. It all starts by exhibiting a genuine and vibrant faith that draws your son to Christ. With God's help you can live in this manner. If God helped me, I know He can help you too. The struggle is real, but you're not alone. God's Spirit is at work in you to will and to work for His good pleasure. Can I get a hallelujah?

THINKING IT THROUGH

What characteristics from your life would you like to see reflected in your son? What can you do to encourage your son to acquire these characteristics?

Psalm 115:3 says, "God is in heaven; He does whatever He pleases." How does this verse influence your concern over your son's future?

LIVING IT OUT

Based on what you learned in this chapter, name one or two ways the Lord has impressed upon you to help your son grow into a man who honors God.

Watch this chapter's video teaching at
www.rhondastoppe.com/books/moms-raising-sons-to-be-men.

CHAPTER 8

TOOLS FOR AUTONOMY

Equipped for Independence

After Brandon graduated from college, Steve and I took him to the airport. With as many earthly possessions as he could fit in his duffle bag and backpack, he moved to Nashville, Tennessee, to work as a guitar technician for the tour of two well-known Christian singers.

Brandon had long dreamed of living in Nashville and using his musical talent in the Christian music industry. Through an amazing series of events, God opened the door for him to do just that. While Steve and I were overjoyed for our son, our tears flowed as we prayed with him, hugged him one last time, and said our good-byes.

I watched Brandon's daddy give him a few final pointers, and kissing his neck, whisper, "Good-bye, son. I am so proud of you. Do well." (Even as I write these words, I am wiping my tears.)

After a time of sniffles and silence during the car ride home, Steve and I were able to talk about how excited we were for Brandon's opportunity, which we are confident was orchestrated by the

Lord's sovereign hand. We humbly celebrated the wonderful man of God Brandon had become. The Lord had certainly given us much grace in raising him. In spite of our less-than-perfect parenting, God had cultivated within our 24-year-old son a love for the Lord and for worship music. By God's grace, my husband and I sent out not a perfect young man, but one who was equipped with the tools to continue growing into a man after God's own heart.

Knowing Your Son

During Brandon's last week at home, I asked, "What is something you would want mothers to know about raising their sons?"

Brandon's response: "Find out who your son is, and train him as an individual. You have to know who he is so you can teach him how to live in obedience to God."

Brandon's comment immediately made me recall a conversation he and I had when he was about 13 years old. He had asked me, "Why won't you guys let me listen to and play whatever music I want? I think I am old enough to decide what music I like."

That's one of those questions where the "because I said so" response would have been the easiest one to give. To answer Brandon's inquiry properly would require some time and interaction on my part. And from Brandon's tone of voice, I knew he was more prepared to argue his case than to receive instruction from his momma.

Though I was pressed for time and not in the mood for a long conversation, I whispered a prayer for wisdom and made a conscious choice, right then and there, to present Brandon with solid and helpful answers to his question.

I began by reminding Brandon of the musical gifts with which God had blessed him. I recalled for him how God had used his infirmity when he was young to mold his talent and love for music—music that honored the Lord.

Now before I go any further, I need to share with you about

something remarkable that had happened to Brandon a few years before this conversation. After Brandon had endured four years of severe seizure activity, and just as many years of us pleading with God to heal our son, Rick, my brother—who was a new believer—had come to visit us. He asked Steve if it would be okay if he prayed for God to heal Brandon.

We knew God *could* heal our boy, but after years of asking, we were not convinced He *would*. However, with faith the size of a mustard seed, we sent Rick up to then-ten-year-old Brandon's room.

Alone upstairs, Brandon and his uncle Ricky prayed a simple prayer for the Lord to heal Brandon. The following morning, Brandon threw his medicine in the garbage and said, "I'm not taking that anymore."

Weeks went by without medicine, then months, and now 20 years later, praise the Lord, Brandon is still seizure-free! God answered the prayer of a little boy and a new believer, and their faith grew beyond measure. (And so did ours!)

Driving the Point Home

On the day Brandon asked about why he could not listen to whatever music he wanted, I reminded him the Lord had healed him for *His* glory, not for Brandon to glorify himself as a musician. I said, "The Lord knows you intimately. He knows what you love. In fact, He put that love within you. God knows what He plans to accomplish through your life with the talents He has given you, which is why He made you the way you are."

I reminded Brandon the Bible teaches that Satan is a liar, a thief who wants to steal, kill, and destroy whatever God might be able to accomplish through our lives. I explained how Satan would love to shatter any hope of his dream coming true by seducing him to pursue the temporal pleasure of playing the world's music.

I pointed Brandon to Jesus's words in Matthew 12:34: "Out of the abundance of the heart the mouth speaks." I explained that whatever Brandon put into his heart would come out of his mouth. As a musician, if Brandon feasted on music celebrating an ungodly life, that would be the kind of music he would sing.

I appealed to the man I knew Brandon wanted to become—one who would honor the Lord. I tried to help him see how sowing seeds of righteousness as a young man would reap God's blessing when he got older. I assured Brandon the Lord wanted to accomplish great things through him, but He could only do so as long as Brandon was obedient. I said, "Brandon, I know you have dreams of being a musician for the Lord. I believe God put that dream within your heart. Would you trade the immediate notoriety of playing at high school dances and nightclubs for a lifetime of playing music God could use to further His kingdom?"

Making a point of looking into Brandon's eyes, I went on: "You are a musician, and you must guard the gift God has given you." I respectfully shared with him how I could see glimpses of what God would accomplish through his obedient life. I realized my job as a parent was to help him see the vision as well—and to help him guard against Satan's attempts to gain a foothold in his life, a foothold that could draw him away from what God had planned for him (Ephesians 4:27).

It has now been two decades since Brandon and I had the conversation about music. Since then, he has earned a college degree in Bible and music, which equipped him to become a worship pastor—the ministry in which he has now served for over a decade. I believe in Brandon's adolescent years, knowing him better than he knew himself was key to having conversations that helped him guard his heart and guide his path.

Now the only reason I was prepared to come alongside of Brandon when he needed wisdom and perspective beyond the advice of his peers was because I had spent time with my son, studied his character, and knew his strengths and weaknesses. I had made a genuine and heartfelt choice to get to know him well.

What about you? Do you spend time with your son to discover who he is?

That brings us to the next of our seven principles:

PRINCIPLE 3: Guide Your Son Toward Independence

When, as a young adult, Brandon stepped out to his new adventure in Nashville, Steve and I had confidence in the man God had grown him to be. We had no reason to fret that Brandon would not be accountable to our watchful eye, for he had been equipped with God's Word and had learned to follow the Lord's leading.

We had seen the evidence of the Holy Spirit at work within Brandon, leading him to obey the Lord and drawing him to repentance when he didn't. With the foundation of God's truth in his heart—a foundation placed there while he was young—Brandon's choices were between him and his Lord. Steve and I changed roles to be his advisors. Our influence now comes through prayer, encouraging words, and advice.

During the years your son is in your home, your goal is to develop a man who is led by the Spirit, who is self-motivated and self-disciplined. Remember, Momma, your goal is not to raise the perfect man, but to raise a man who knows how to recover from his mistakes so he is equipped to repent and continue on his path of following Christ. You have a little less than two decades to train him to depend upon God and not you. Controlling his every move is not the way to prepare your son for manhood. I have witnessed more than a few mothers who so control their sons that they prevent them from developing independence.

If you have had a significant controlling influence in the events and decisions of your son's life, maybe you need to evaluate *why* his "perfect obedience" to your wishes is so important to you, and whether you might be inhibiting his ability to become his own man and make right decisions for himself.

Evaluate Your Motives

When I first became a mother, I was determined not to have kids who were out of control. I wanted to be respected as a good mother and not known as someone who had unmanageable children. One day I overreacted when one of our kids skipped and laughed through the sanctuary after church.

Vaughn, one of my mentors, asked me why I had reacted so strongly. He made me evaluate my reason for my "be quiet in the sanctuary" rule. Through a series of questions, Vaughn helped me see my motivation was not based on a strong conviction that my children honor the house of the Lord, but more on a concern for what others would think of me as a mother. Vaughn said, "Never enforce standards on your child based upon what other people think. Determine the rules founded upon commands in the Bible and the leading of the Holy Spirit. Hold your child to the principles of the Lord, *not the standards of people.* By your example, you will train them to be God-pleasers rather than people-pleasers."

After some serious soul searching, I had to admit the number one reason I wanted well-behaved children was I wanted others to think highly of me. Vaughn's honest yet painful words had convicted me of a sin to which I was completely oblivious. (One very good reason to invite mature mentors into your life.) With my own tendency toward people-pleasing, I probably would not have recognized my wrong motive until I had thoroughly ruined my children.

While having obedient children is a delight, you must evaluate the reason you want your kids to obey. Have you made the respect of others an idol within your heart? If you have become harsh, anxious, or controlling as a parent, you would do well to repent and ask the Lord to show you how to establish new patterns of parenting. The Holy Spirit can help you selflessly love your children with a love that centers on pleasing God and not others—as well as a love that seeks your children's good above your own.

Why You Can't Protect Him from Error

Every mother hopes her son will make right decisions so he never has to feel the painful consequences of failure. However, if you closely rule over every nuance of your son's decision-making, he may not learn how to properly recover from his mistakes. As your son matures, rather than micromanaging his every decision, create an environment with opportunities for your son to make choices—and sometimes fail. Giving your son an element of freedom, within loving boundaries, will allow him room to learn how to govern himself as an adult under God's authority. And in those times when your son does sin, you will have the opportunity to teach him how to repent and recover from incorrect choices.

Whenever infractions occur, if you determine to see them as chances to teach your son how to find his way back from choosing the wrong path, you will be less likely to take personal offense to his failure. As you ask your son the right questions, the Lord can help you discern whether his actions come from a defiant heart or are simply immature mistakes. That, in turn, will help you to implement consequences that suit the transgression.

While your son matures into a man, he is striving to interpret all he experiences. The way you react to him when he confesses his wrongdoings can influence his interpretation of how God responds to him when he repents. The Bible says God's mercy toward those who fear Him is great, and it reminds us that He knows how frail we are (Psalm 103:11-14). Will you determine to respond with kind discipline and mercy when your son sins?

The opposite extreme of a controlling mother is one who remains completely uninvolved in disciplining or directing her son. Rather than confront their sons, many mothers make the mistake of granting complete autonomy once they reach puberty—only to find

There is a war raging for your son's heart. Satan will use any means necessary to seduce him. Your son needs your godly, wise influence in his life. Mom, you must engage in the battle.

them seeking significance from their peers, choosing a path of destruction.

There is a war raging for your son's heart. Satan will use any means necessary to seduce him. Your son needs your godly, wise influence in his life. Mom, you must engage in the battle. If you don't, you are neglecting the calling God has given you.

Although your son may resist your authority while he is an adolescent, he desperately needs to know he can trust you to uphold the godly rules you established while he was young. The boundaries you define will offer stability to your son amid the insecurity of puberty.

The Process of Repentance

When your son comes to you contrite over his bad decisions, be careful to learn from God's pattern of balancing judgment with mercy. As you encourage him for having the courage to come to you and confess, walk your son through the process of repentance to the Lord.

Does your son agree with God that his action was wrong? Help your son move past the "I'm sorry I did this because the consequences stink" response.

Encourage your son to confess to the Lord that he has sinned against Him. Help him understand that the greatest problem with his action was that it was committed against the Lord.

Teach your son that to repent means to turn from your sin. To assure your son will truly change, help him see the need to remove himself from anything that will lead him to commit that same sin again.

Then, just as God promises not to remember the transgressions of a repentant soul, once the appropriate consequence has been imposed, determine not to bring up past failures each time your son makes a wrong choice.

If your son does not willingly come to you to confess an infraction, follow the Lord's example in the garden of Eden. God knew of Adam and Eve's sin. They hid themselves, but He sought them out, asked them questions to make them see their wicked ways, and then imposed the consequences for their sin, followed with the promise of a way to redemption.

God will mercifully forgive and forget the sins of a repentant person, but He will not remove the repercussions of their sinful actions. Follow the Lord's example by gracefully and consistently imposing consequences that help your son realize there are always ramifications for wrong actions. Ask the Lord to give you compassion for your son's frailty, coupled with a steady discipline that does not overlook his infractions.

Rite of Passage

Learning to walk with your son through the rocky road of his teens is not for the faint of heart. This season requires God's wisdom. The Bible says, "If any of you lacks wisdom, let him ask of God, who gives to all liberally and without reproach, and it will be given to him" (James 1:5). If you learn to rely on wisdom from God's Word rather than earthly wisdom or your own emotions, you will illuminate an unwavering path for your son through a difficult season.

In some cultures, boys leave on walkabout, kill an animal, or trudge over hot coals to proclaim their unquestionable arrival into manhood. I firmly believe adolescent boys long for a sort of line-drawn-in-the-sand "event" that declares they are now a man.

Unfortunately, our society offers no particular ritual. All they have is the unwritten code among men, "Don't be a momma's boy." Repeatedly I have observed a once-compliant, tender boy become resistant to his mother's rule, even growing defiant and rebellious as he attempts to be recognized as a man. And all too often I have seen mothers try to force their sons to remain a *good little boy* when they are aching to be respected as adults. Sadly, the more these alarmed mothers tighten their grips, the more their sons slip through their fingers.

As strongly as I know how, I want to encourage you to make a conscious effort to show your son that you see him becoming a man—or he will fight you to prove it. If your son's father is in the home, consider decisively removing yourself from the ultimate authority over him. In the previous chapter, I shared the story of Brandon becoming the ditch digger. The specific transfer of authority from mother to father transformed my relationship with my adolescent son.

As a young teen, Brandon would sometimes come back to me, rather than his father, to ask permission to go places or be involved in activities (usually because he thought he could persuade me to say yes when he knew his father would say no). Sometimes it was all I could do not to make the decision. However, Steve and I had agreed to transfer all decisions concerning Brandon to him so that I could say, "I have an agreement with your father that I am unwilling to break." To honor my husband's authority, I faithfully directed Brandon to his father whenever he had a request. In so doing, I influenced my son's respect for his father as well.

I know, some of you are fearfully gasping at the thought of loosening your grip on your little boy. You are mumbling something like, "You don't know my husband." But I am telling you, I have seen miraculous transformation in adolescent boys whose good-willed fathers stepped up to the transfer of authority. But please heed this warning: If you take this great step, do not take back control whenever you feel your husband is not measuring up to your parenting ideals. All disagreements should be discussed in private, away from the ears of your children. And you must be willing to submit to your husband's final decisions concerning your son.

Believe me, you will do more harm than good if you disrespect your husband's authority in front of your son. When a child is caught between the conflicting authorities of his parents, he ends up losing respect for *both* of them. An expert in child development says the most hostile, aggressive teenagers he has known have emerged from this kind of backdrop.[1]

I will go one step further: Not only should you honor your husband's authority over your son, but you should work very hard to celebrate all of your husband's wonderful attributes to your son. Young men need heroes they can look up to. All too often, mothers rob their sons of the wonderful experience of admiring their father because they continually point out their husband's shortcomings. As you esteem your husband's position to lead your family, your son will likely follow your lead and respect him as well.

I have never felt so free as when my husband *rescued* me from the daily power struggle between me and my adolescent son. My consistent response—"Ask your father"—eliminated many conflicts between me and Brandon. Our relationship quickly developed as I respected the man Brandon was becoming, and Brandon lovingly protected and helped me with tasks that were too much for me. I remember purposefully asking Brandon to go outside to check why the dogs were barking and asking him to help me lift a five-gallon water jug because he was stronger than I was. Brandon's countenance would visibly change as he responded to my request. With his shoulders set and his chest pushed out, he took on the role of man-of-the-house while his father was away at work. The more I deferred to Brandon as a man, the more he rose to the occasion. This was, without a doubt, a defining decision for my relationship with my son.

Single mother, please don't lose heart. God promises to be Father to the fatherless (Psalm 68:5). He is able to raise up godly men in your family or church family to mentor and guide your son toward independence from you and dependence upon Christ alone. For example, God brought our son Tony to our family as an adolescent boy in need of a godly father. In the same way, Timothy was just a teen when God raised up the apostle Paul to train him in godliness. In the end, Paul handed the very mantle of his ministry over to his son-in-the-faith. And God can do the same for your son too.

Your Son's Identity in Christ

To prepare your son for autonomy, you would do well to create an environment for him to learn to know himself biblically. Spending time developing your son's identity, based upon *who he is in Christ*, will equip him to leave your home with God-centered character, strength, purpose, and confidence in Christ. Of course, before you can do this, it's necessary for you to understand your identity in Christ as well.

Your son is growing up in a culture more concerned about a good self-image and personal happiness than about what is right or wrong. In other words, self comes first—and this, in turn, tends to nurture self-pride. Ultimately, thinking highly of oneself is nothing more than self-worship—in a word, idolatry. Romans 12:3 warns that a Christian should not "think of himself more highly than he ought to think."

Use the Bible to give your son a proper, God-honoring image of himself. Second Peter 1:3-9 teaches that believers have everything needed for life and godliness, through their knowledge of Christ. And the passage also warns that Christians can become ineffective and unproductive by forgetting who they are in their relationship to Jesus.

In his book *Instruments in the Redeemer's Hands*, Paul David Tripp says, "The gospel identity and its amazing resources are a powerful defense in the war for our hearts...The war for the heart is a war of identity. How people respond to Satan's attack depends on the identity they have embraced...[The enemy] wins daily skirmishes with us by clouding or attacking our identity."[2]

Do not minimize the importance of training your son to

establish his identity in a relationship with Jesus Christ. If your son is a believer, he has been given everything he needs to live a God-honoring life. Teach him to see himself through the resources afforded to him by the gospel, and you will equip him to stand against peer pressure, his own fleshly desires, and Satan's attacks. Satan cannot be victorious against anyone who takes to heart, and lives, the message of identity defined in 2 Peter 1:3-9.

When your son has a biblical understanding of who he is in Christ, he will be prepared to withstand peer pressure and discern right choices as a man. If you determine to allow your son enough freedom to practice making wise decisions and kindly correct him when he fails, you will teach him how to repent when he sins. While he is an adolescent, work to discover ways to *hand him his adulthood*. Doing this will provide your son with a foundation for *independence* from you and *dependence* upon Christ. In this way you can have a tremendously positive influence upon your son, and ultimately, upon the generation he will influence.

THINKING IT THROUGH

Read 2 Peter 1:3-9. What are some ways you can help your son develop his identity in Christ? Put another way, what does he need to know?

From what you learned in this chapter, write out two or three things you can do in the upcoming days and weeks to build your relationship with your son.

LIVING IT OUT

Do you worry about what others think about you as a parent? Is it possible you have somehow made the opinion of others an idol? Take some time to prayerfully consider your motivations before the Lord. In the space below, write a prayer asking the Lord to purify your heart and your motives.

Watch this chapter's video teaching at
www.rhondastoppe.com/books/moms-raising-sons-to-be-men.

CHAPTER 9

THE ART OF INTIMACY

Get Acquainted with His Heart

When Barry was in middle school, his father lost his position as youth pastor at their church. The heartache and disappointment his father experienced reverberated through their family.

Barry's mother, Georgene, determined to draw near to the Lord amid the trial. Her faithful response made a strong impression on each of her five children. Barry said about his mother: "The moment in which my mother had the greatest influence on my life was when I was in the seventh grade, and my dad had been severely hurt in the ministry and found himself jumping from job to job. In frustration I asked, 'Why doesn't God do something to help Dad?' My mother could tell that I was getting upset with God. With tears running down her cheeks, she cried out, 'Lord, please protect my son from becoming bitter toward You.' I absolutely believe that I would have never become a pastor if she had answered me out of the deep hurt in her heart."

This painful experience at a vulnerable age could have sent Barry into rebellion against God. Had Georgene wallowed in her sorrow, voiced angry disappointment to her family, or focused upon the circumstances rather than God, she probably would have lost sight of her ministry to her children. And she likely would have forfeited the opportunity to point Barry in the right direction. Amid difficult trials, Georgene's sincere faith and godly relationship with her son helped her to mold him into a man who would go on to serve the Lord.

Just as Barry could trust his mother's advice because she lived the message she taught, so you will earn the confidence of your son if you display genuine faith in God. When you react to life's circumstances with a calm assurance in the Lord, you will do more to validate your testimony to your son than your words ever could. Have you ever considered that the Lord may allow you to go through trials to validate your testimony to your children?

The Examined Life

An unexamined life is a careless life. Your son will not know how to analyze his behavior unless you teach him. So learn to appraise yourself by evaluating the reasons for your responses to whatever life brings your way.

As your son watches you practice godly self-examination, he will then learn how to discern the reasons for his responses to people and circumstances in life. Training your son to think about *why* he reacts in certain ways will lay a foundation for true change. When you help your son examine his heart and see his thoughts and actions the way God sees them, he will begin to understand why his behavior *and* thinking need to change.

There is little time to waste. Determine to live deliberately, and not to let each day just happen. Spend time with other mothers who have the same sense of urgency to mold the character of their children. As you go about your day, remember that your son is observing how you live. He is studying your words, actions, and attitudes to discern whether your relationship with Christ is for real.

God expects you to devote your life to making much of Him. Apathy is your enemy. If your words and actions are filled with a passion to share Christ and to encourage others, your excitement will be contagious to your son. Your example will teach him the normal Christian life is one of urgent service to God. And you will expose him to the idea that *serving God is an exciting way of life.*

There is no time to waste, for in just a few years your son will become a man. Life is short, and childhood is short. So weigh the use of the time you have with your son (Psalm 90:12). You're not just changing diapers, burping him, and attending his school and sports events. You are representing Christ to your son, which influences not only him but everyone he meets in the future!

Let's look at the next principle for effective parenting, which addresses how you can develop a solid connection with your son.

PRINCIPLE 4: Knowing Your Son Well Allows You to Encourage His Strengths and Correct His Weaknesses

It has been said, "No one cares what you know until they know you care." If you want to be heard by your son, he must believe you genuinely care about him. If he doesn't sense you care, he will reject you and refuse your instruction. Be willing to invest the time required to build a close relationship with him. And listen—*really* listen—when he talks.

The best way you can learn about your son's strengths and weaknesses, and his hopes and dreams, is to spend *quantity* time with him. Not just quality time—the times when you engage on a deep heart-to-heart level. There's no substitute for the quantity of normal, day-to-day doing-life hours your son needs from you.

When my younger daughter Kayla started kindergarten, I went back to work full-time. I tried very hard to balance my job with raising my children. Each day after school, the bus dropped Kayla and her brother off at my office. All in all, it seemed like a perfect arrangement. As the school year went on, however, Brandon, my quiet one, became quieter. He lost himself in LEGOs and videos. Kayla, on the other hand, grew quite demanding, and because I was tired from working all day, I gradually developed a habit of giving in to her.

By the time the second semester rolled around, I no longer knew the names of Brandon's friends at school. And each evening, as I gave Kayla her bath, she would make an effort to talk with me about her day. I clearly remember one day she was particularly animated as she told me a story about something that had happened on the playground. I was tired and trying to wash her hair. As she chattered on, I grew irritated that she wouldn't stop talking so I could rinse the soap off her face.

Then it hit me: I had become so consumed with work I had forgotten my *real calling* was to be this precious little girl's mommy! To look her in the eyes, listen to every detail about every person she played with that day—what kind of shoes they wore and how they did their hair.

After I tucked my cute little chatterbox into bed, I went downstairs in tears and told Steve how much I had gotten off track. We knew we could not afford for me to quit working, but we decided to do whatever necessary so I could resign. I worked through the rest of the school year making adjustments in our budget and finding a side hustle to help with our finances so we could prepare for my eventual unemployment.

That summer, my children were overjoyed to have their mommy back! As I say this, I am not trying to make working mothers feel guilty, or to call all mothers to stay at home. If you *need* to work, then ask the Lord to provide you the strength and time that will enable you to enjoy meaningful interaction with your children. I know many working mothers who have raised wonderful, godly children. And with God's help I believe you can too.

And if you are a stay-at-home or work-from-home mom, don't let opportunities for in-depth time with your son slip by. Without any effort on your part to have purposeful interaction with your son, you will not develop a good relationship with him. So determine to schedule time during which your sole focus is him, and nothing else.

Develop ways to know your son. He'll invite you into his world if he knows you're genuinely interested! Ask him specific questions about what's going on in his life—his accomplishments, struggles, goals, fears, relationships, and dreams.

And don't forget to dream with him. Men tend to talk about their dreams as if they will attempt to carry them out. So you would be wise to allow your son to speak about his dreams without shooting "reality" into his plans. Enjoy him as he shares his ambitions. There will be plenty of time to talk to him later about the dangers or challenges of specific opportunities—if he ever actually pursues them. When you allow your son to share his dreams openly, you are laying the groundwork for him to share other hopes and dreams with you in the future.

When women visit together, they often sit across from each other, focusing directly on the conversation at hand. By contrast, men tend to communicate side by side, often while doing a task at the same time. If you want to get your son talking, remind yourself that his communication tendencies are likely different from yours. So when you want to talk, sit next to him when he is doing something he loves to do. Find ways to be involved in his activity.

Some of my best opportunities to talk with our older son, Tony, came while I sat in his Jeep as he worked on it. With his eyes focused on the engine, we talked about girls, his dream of becoming a fighter pilot, girls, his college aspirations—and did I mention we talked about girls?

Shoulder to shoulder, we connected as Tony's mind and heart were engaged in our conversations. I am certain if I had forced Tony to sit across from me and share his deepest thoughts I would have heard not a word. And for my younger son, Brandon, we had the best shoulder-to-shoulder conversations while he was learning to drive.

Take a moment to consider how you might best enter your teenaged son's world to create an atmosphere of connection. If your son has a habit of disappearing to play with toys, follow him to his room sometime. Ask if he wouldn't mind if you watched for a while. Yes, even if that means hours of observing him play with his LEGOs. Recently my son Brandon and his son, Ledger, built a LEGO Millennium Falcon. I was impressed with my daughter-in-law Jessy's patience as she sat nearby for the 17 hours it took them to build the monstrosity. Alongside her men, Jessy was afforded opportunities for great conversations.

And as he plays, don't use that time to talk about all that is on your mind. Rather, *make yourself listen*. Long periods of silence are okay; don't feel you must fill the quiet with words. Or ask him just one thought-provoking question and see where he takes the conversation. Keep in mind you are there to observe, encourage, and maybe engage in his activity—not criticize how he plays or clean up after him.

Although it might be hard for you to find time to do this because you have so many other pressing demands, be careful you do not miss opportunities to get acquainted with your son's heart. Remember, there is an *urgency* to build this relationship. Your son will soon be grown, and the foundation you take time to lay now will stand firm for years to come.

The mother of my precious son-in-law, Estevan, entered his world by playing video games with him. He has fond memories of the hours they spent together. When-ever Estevan speaks of those times with his mom, his eyes light up and he smiles. Sadly, Estevan's mother died unexpectedly during his senior year of high school. The time she spent simply enjoying the company of her son went on to leave a lasting impression upon him. In this case, time spent in front of video games was definitely not wasted!

> There is an *urgency* to build this relationship. Your son will soon be grown, and the foundation you take time to lay now will stand firm for years to come.

Whether your son is an athlete, spelling bee champion, musician, or computer whiz, if you make a habit of spending time alongside him and applaud-ing his accomplishments, you will become an important part of his world. Your effort will say to him, "I value you, so I value what's important to you."

Hear Out His Struggles

When your son opens the window of his heart and shares about his struggles, be careful not to talk over him in an attempt to resolve his issues. The danger of speaking over your son with all the answers is you end up not taking time to just listen. I have watched Brandon start to tell me about something with which he struggles, only to shut down when I begin throwing quick-fix answers at him. Proverbs 18:2 says, "A fool has no delight in understanding, but in expressing his own heart." Waiting for my son to take a breath so I can speak my mind, I have played the fool more times than I care to count!

If you really want to connect with your son, invite him to tell you what is troubling him by asking him to help you understand how he is feeling. Then wait for him to talk. It's possible your son may not even know exactly how he feels until he hears himself talk about what's going through his mind.

Though many of the issues your son faces may seem trivial to you, do not minimize the impact they are having upon him. Saying things like, "It's not that big of a deal; someday you won't even remember this," will only serve to put a barrier between you and your son—and likely send him looking for encouragement from another source. You can encourage him by listening carefully, then acknowledging how he is feeling and gently offering words of hope, encouragement, and direction.

If your son is upset with a specific person, prayerfully consider how you can help him see *his own contribution* to the struggle. (There are always two sides to a problem.) Don't be the mom who constantly blames others for her son's conflicts. We have all met the mother who goes rushing into the classroom claiming her son is the victim of everyone else's wrongdoing.

Even if the conflict appears to be one-sided, teach your son how to forgive the person who has wronged him—whether or not the other person asks for forgiveness. Teach your son how pardoning another person's offense will free him from becoming bitter. Explain to him that holding on to resentment will certainly quench the Holy Spirit in his life and hinder his walk with Christ.

If you constantly intervene when others do your son wrongly, you will waste valuable opportunities to train him to deal with conflict honorably. As a rule, resentful people sow seeds of resentment in their children. And forgiving people raise forgiving children. Focus on living as a godly example before your son, and you will teach him how to handle discord properly.

Your home should *not* be characterized by conflict. If your son is exposed to fighting and arguing within the home, this will become the way in which he will relate to others. The habits he sees on display in his relationships at home will spill over into his friendships, his marriage, and one day, his parenting. Has it ever occurred to you that you are raising the father of your grandchildren?

Many people allow their children to fight and argue, giving the excuse, "All kids fight." But the Bible says love is kind and long-suffering, and the follower of God is not quarrelsome. Yes, all siblings will have conflicts. But you, as a parent, have the unique privilege of training your children to talk through their disagreements in a calm, kind manner and come to reasonable resolutions. You are responsible before the Lord to train your son not to develop quarrelsome habits.

Our two youngest children, Brandon and Kayla, are two years apart. When they were old enough to begin fighting over their toys, I was going a bit stir-crazy running interference for every argument. You know what I'm talking about: "Who had it first? Give that back to your sister. Don't take that from your brother."

One day I watched a documentary about sibling rivalry. In the documentary, siblings who were prone to fighting were placed in a room without a parent present. During that time, the children played graciously with each other. But as soon as Mom entered the room, the fighting began. Their mother attempted to bring peace and justice to their conflict. Amazingly, as soon the mother left the room, the siblings went back to playing peacefully.

In numerous case studies, different siblings displayed the same behavior. Researchers have determined that for some reason, the children enjoyed involving their mother in their disputes. It was almost like a game where each child would try to "win" their mother's defense. When mother would defend one child, he would "get a point." And when mother came to the aid of the other child, she was "awarded a point." The show ended by hinting that mothers would do well to allow their children to resolve their own struggles without getting involved, thus removing the children's motivation to argue.

I decided I wanted to test this concept but add a biblical perspective to it. I told my children, "Ephesians 4:32 says, 'Be kind one to another.' God commands it. So if you fight or argue, you are disobeying God." I apologized to Kayla and Brandon for having gotten involved in their past conflicts, and informed them that from now on, I would not engage in their arguments. I added, "The rule of this house is no fighting, so there will be consequences if you do not resolve conflicts quietly and respectfully." I *promised* Kayla and Brandon I would take away any toy they argued over, without asking who was at fault. As far as I was concerned, my goal was to teach them to honor the Lord in their relationship by not fighting, not to administer justice every time they disagreed with each other.

Soon I had to make good on my promise, so I went upstairs to take away the toy the two children were struggling over. They were stunned and pleaded with me to let them keep the toy. I said, "I can't. Remember, I made you a promise. I have to keep my word."

I was determined to have peace in my home, so I stuck with my newfound concept. Within a very short time, my children stopped bickering. Whenever I would hear their voices get intense over a toy, I would call out my familiar mantra, "Work it out." I would then hear them start to whisper things like, "She's gonna come take it away! All right, you have a turn." I know, the whole thing sounds so simple, but to enforce this new way of life required a lot of discipline on my part to change an all-too-set habit.

Peace reigned between Kayla and Brandon until the two reached adolescence. Then their conflicts were not about toys, but about something one said to the other. One of their biggest conflicts came when Brandon's best friend began to have feelings for Kayla. Since Brandon felt that Estevan had broken the "bro code" and Kayla seemed to care less about how Brandon felt, they had to work through some pretty hurtful conversations. Eventually, Kayla and Estevan grew up and got married. And now Brandon is thrilled that his best friend is also his brother-in-law.

Of course Brandon and Kayla's arguments were magnified by the hormonal mood swings adolescents are known for. My husband and I modified the consequence of taking away the toy to not allowing them to talk to each other. Because they were best friends, the punishment was excruciating—especially for Kayla, who loved to talk! The last time we imposed the don't-talk-to-each-other rule, Kayla and Brandon were grounded from speaking to each other for a whole month. What a long month it was—for *all* of us! But the end result was peaceful communication between my two adolescent children.

Know His Friends

Your son will not develop social graces on his own. He will talk too loud, laugh rudely at inappropriate moments, finish the last cookie, and be selfish toward his friends. If you do not train him how to interact socially, he will be left to figure out for himself what works and what does not. I am always surprised when mothers complain about their sons' inappropriate behaviors, yet at the same time they neglect to teach them positive alternatives.

While having your son's friends over for a visit may take up your time and bring wear and tear to your house, each time this happens you are graced with the opportunity to observe your son's conduct within his relationships. Did you notice I used the word *observe*?

As you watch your son interact with his friends, make mental notes of behaviors he may need to modify. Don't intervene right away. Instead, wait for an opportunity when the two of you are alone. Then talk to your son and help him think through how he might be making others feel when he engages in unsuitable actions. It's important that you determine to base your concerns on what the Bible says about your son's behavior, for that will help you guard from nitpicking over every little thing that may have bothered you. Make sure you talk about real heart issues, and not just little things that get on your nerves. Allowing for your son's immaturity, address only what you are convinced will help build his social skills and mold his character so he will grow more Christlike.

Most important of all, you are more likely to get a favorable response from your son when you treat him with respect and deal with your concerns when you two are alone. If you admonish your son in front of his friends or try to manipulate his behavior by embarrassing him, I guarantee his buddies will not want to hang out at your house anymore. They will be humiliated for him. And your son will feel betrayed by you and will not trust how you might treat him in front of his peers. If you publicly dishonor your son, you will only serve to alienate him from yourself.

So what should you do if a behavior must be addressed while your son's friends are visiting? Quietly pull him aside and ask him to make the adjustment. Do this in a way that doesn't call attention to what is happening. Your son will appreciate your sensitivity and your loyalty.

Finally, realize there is wisdom in waiting for the right time to talk with your son about social manners. If you pounce on him with a list of criticisms as soon as everyone has gone home, he may end up tuning you out. Rather, pray for opportunities to bring up your concerns at the right times, in ways he will understand are for God's glory and his own betterment. Taking time to teach your son how to be a good and loyal friend will help him honor the Lord with his relationships and become someone people trust and genuinely like.

Guard His Heart

In these days of social media and cell phones, your son will likely ask for his own phone. Even if other kids his age are given phones, don't bend to peer pressure to give your a son a phone at an early age. There is much evidence to support the negative influence cell phone usage has upon children.

Dr. James Dobson observes: "Are you aware that the average person between the ages of eight and eighteen spends approximately 44.5 hours each week engaging with some form of media? That's the equivalent of a full-time job and several hours of overtime! With consumption at this level, it's little wonder that media has become a type of 'super-peer,' influencing behaviors and shaping values."[1]

With these concerns in mind, if at some point you do allow your son to have his own phone and social media accounts, be aware how much of his social interaction will become virtual, which can hamper his development to communicate in person. Young people miss out on learning the art of good communication when they rely heavily on texting, messaging, and social media comments. Most parents would agree that giving a child free access to the internet is a recipe for disaster. However, once you allow your children to have social media accounts, it's easy to let your guard down and grow unaware of the amount of time they spend online. Which means they spend less time engaging with you or their siblings. And the unsupervised time your son spends interacting virtually will influence his worldview, while creating in him anxiety and dread. Home is no longer a safe haven when, for example, the "mean girls" are no longer only bothersome at school; now they can find their way into your son's safe place at home to ridicule, manipulate, or undermine him in his virtual community.

You have every right to set up restrictions or revoke online privileges if your son abuses them. I am continually amazed at how many mothers complain about what their sons expose themselves to online, yet it never occurs to them to monitor their internet usage.

A word of caution: If you do not supervise your son's internet usage, he *will* be exposed to pornography. Your son is not mature enough to realize the danger. So you must not be unaware of Satan's schemes. The enemy comes to steal, kill, and destroy your child's morality. And Satan will use any means available to draw your son into the clutches of pornography addiction. The best way to keep your son from becoming addicted to pornography is to teach him how and *why* to guard himself, *before* he finds himself in its clutches.

A reasonable way to protect your son from the seductions he may find online is to require him to spend his internet time in an area where other members of the family are present, rather than alone in his room or bathroom. This could include a house rule that all cell phones will be left in a central location overnight—and not taken to their bedrooms.

You can see the importance of protecting your young son's mind from being influenced by pornography. The world may say, "Boys will be boys," and that viewing porn is just normal behavior, but you must be aware of the terrible hold this practice will have upon your impressionable son—a hold that he will likely battle for the rest of his life. A door open to online pornography will not close easily.

Do not be deceived into thinking pornography is not destructive to your son emotionally, physically, and spiritually. Scripture is clear on this; 1 Thessalonians 4:3 urges believers to avoid sexual immorality, and a few verses later, Paul writes, "God did not call us to uncleanness, but in holiness" (verse 7). First Corinthians 6:18-20 says to flee sexual immorality, for a Christian's body belongs to God. And Hebrews 13:4 says to keep the marriage bed undefiled. The shameful practices involving pornographic material will sow seeds of destruction in your son's life, and indulging in porn will steal from him the pleasure of his marriage bed. You, who are wise and led by the Lord, must not look the other way in this matter.

My son-in-law, Jacob Ebner, has counseled many young men who struggle with pornography, so I asked him if he could share some insights for mothers regarding this sensitive issue. Here is his response:

> The reason porn is so destructive to your son's body, heart, and relationship with Christ can be found in 1 Corinthians 6, where we learn that the body is a temple of the Holy Spirit. Sexual sin is sin against the body, and since the body houses the Spirit, sexual sin therefore grieves the Spirit. Pornography presumes that a person has full rights to his own body to do with it whatever he pleases. Whether it be looking with lust on a woman and therefore committing adultery in one's heart or indulging in illicit sex of any kind, it is treating the blood of Christ with contempt because we have been bought with a price. We are no longer our own; therefore, we are called to glorify Christ with our bodies. Our bodies are to be instruments of righteousness, not wickedness, because we use our physical bodies to worship God.
>
> Pornography offers a cheap counterfeit of what God has

intended for marriage and sex to be, which is a representation of Christ's marriage to His bride, and His love for the church. Christ's desire is that the church, His bride, be presented to Him as pure and spotless, washed by His blood. This is our ultimate motivation to remain pure in all that we do. (See Romans 6; 12:1-2; 1 Thessalonians 4:3-8.)

Although the world says there is no harm in allowing your son to indulge in pornography, you would do well to consider God's warning in Proverbs 22:8: "He who sows iniquity will reap sorrow." God has given you the responsibility of training your son to guard his young and impressionable heart. So respectfully teach him the far-reaching consequences of pornography, and the rewards of pursuing holiness.

As your son wrestles with the deeper issues of life, he wants to believe you are *for him* rather than against him. Consider how you can best train, motivate, and inspire him by devoting yourself to intentionally studying his character and listening to him. The time you invest in building a close relationship with your son will knit his heart to yours, and in time, you will win his trust. Earn your son's trust, and he will reward you the honorable position of confidante and counselor as you guide him more and more toward independence.

THINKING IT THROUGH

Read 1 Corinthians 7:17. What are some ways that viewing motherhood as God's call on your life will change the way you parent your son?

LIVING IT OUT

Write out and memorize Galatians 2:16. How does this verse say a person is justified? What does it say about trying to be justified by works? How will you teach the message of Galatians 2:16 to your son?

Watch this chapter's video teaching at
www.rhondastoppe.com/books/moms-raising-sons-to-be-men.

CHAPTER 10

CONVERSATIONS THAT MATTER

How to Talk So He Will Listen

You are so lazy. You'll never amount to anything!" Because Carl's mother had said those words to him so many times, he had long ago accepted them as true and lost his incentive to try to please her. Carl's father, meanwhile, was an abusive alcoholic who never offered any words of encouragement.

The summer Carl turned 15, he went to visit his uncle's ranch. He admired the gruff old cowboy and wanted very much to gain his approval. During the time Carl worked on the ranch, he found great satisfaction at the end of each day when his uncle, a man of few words, would say the phrase he'd grown to love: "Boy, you done good."

Carl says, "Those summers I spent with my uncle transformed me. Though he spoke very little, what he did say made me *believe* I had value. I owe my success in life to that old cowboy."

Proverbs 18:21 declares, "Death and life are in the power of the tongue." Have you ever considered how powerfully your words influence your son? You have been blessed with the wonderful task of training, teaching, correcting, and encouraging your son—so choose your words carefully.

Good dialogue is an essential part of training your son to be a godly man, and this brings us to our next principle, which will deal with practical ways you can develop better communication with your son.

PRINCIPLE 5: Talk So Your Son Listens, and Listen So He Talks

———

Learning to speak to your son in ways he will pay attention to what you have to say will require effort on your part. But it's an effort that will bear tremendous rewards. Here are some useful tips you'll want to apply as you pave the way to good communication.

1. Involve Your Son's Emotions

"The most effective communication always includes an emotional ingredient—the *feeling* factor, the *excitement* element," writes Dr. Howard Hendricks.[1] So when you talk to your son about important issues, infuse your conversation with elements that will help involve his emotions.

Using stories and word pictures is a great way to touch on the feelings of a listener. For example, if your son tends to ignore his younger brother, you might tell your son a story like this: "Imagine you are on a basketball team. You like all your teammates, but you especially look up to the star player. However, whenever you try to talk to him, he refuses to listen. And when you try to get his attention by doing nice things for him, he ignores your efforts. How would that make you feel?" After your son talks about how the rejection might affect him, you can say, "That is how you make your little brother feel every time you treat him like he is insignificant."

When you get your son to *feel* the impact of his actions on his little brother, he is more likely to adjust how he treats him.

2. Engage Your Son's Intellect

Help your son understand your point by giving him logical reasoning he can follow. Teach your son to think through the views you present and how to respond after intelligently considering your message. To influence your son with your message, he must believe you are passionately convinced your ideas are worthwhile. When your son sees you genuinely believe in your principles, and he can logically discern how they work for you, he will be drawn to consider your message.

3. Develop Shared Interests with Your Son

This practice will also lay the foundation for good communication. So make it your goal to establish things in common with your son. The more you understand his interests—the thoughts and activities that captivate him and fill his imagination—the more excitement he'll have in conversing with you about them. If you dismiss whatever intrigues him, ultimately, he will feel dismissed by you as well. And the best way to figure out what intrigues him is to...

4. Ask Your Son Questions

Your son holds thoughts in his heart. Asking pertinent questions will show your son you are genuinely interested in who he is and what he is thinking and help you understand his motivations and concerns. By making statements like, "Help me understand how you feel about that. What happened next? How did it make you feel when that happened?" you will show your son you are attentive and genuinely engaged in the conversation.

Not only will making inquiries encourage your son to share his stories with you; it will also help you learn how he responds to life and to other people.

5. Listen Well

Everyone longs to be heard by the people who are important to them. When you listen to your son, you send the message that he is significant and valuable, and that what he says matters to you. As he talks about events, make a mental note of names and reactions of people in the story. Remembering details—such as his friends' names— shows your son you are attentive when he talks. It tells your son, "Your relationships matter to me."

Your attentive listening will establish an atmosphere that will encourage future conversations. And in doing so, you'll have further opportunities to teach your son a biblical worldview, or a biblical way to interact with his world.

6. Delight in Your Son

Enjoy your son by learning to delight in who he is. Delight is just one way of expressing your love for him! Laugh at your son's jokes, cheer him on, cry with him. *Feel what he feels.* When something exciting happens, be the person your son cannot wait to share his experience with. By making an effort to express approval and delight in your son, you will encourage him to communicate with you, and you will naturally open up opportunities to guide him with God's truth.

7. Be Joyful

Would your son use the word *joyful* to describe your family? Nehemiah 8:10 promises, "The joy of the LORD is your strength." I know one mother whose husband was terribly harsh to her son. In spite of the father's overshadowing hostility, she determined to let the Lord's joy strengthen her. Her son, who is now an adult, says his mother's joy amid tumultuous times was a beacon of light that gave him hope and directed him to Christ.

No matter how difficult life becomes, you can cultivate a happy heart by talking about the many blessings found in Christ. And by example you can teach your son to celebrate the life, joy, and purpose found in a relationship with Jesus Christ. If you determine to rejoice about even the simplest favors from the Lord, you will sow seeds of joy in your family and form a secure base for godly communication.

8. Teach Him to Communicate

If your son is not a big talker, look for opportune times to ask him questions that might encourage him to open up. Try asking him questions like, "What is one thing you are struggling with right now?" or "Why is John your best friend?" or "What is your favorite thing about school?" Give your son time to think before he speaks. Don't answer the question for him. If he is unable to put his response into words, you could casually present him with some multiple-choice answers. But again, give him time to respond.

You can also teach your son how to talk in a way that will hold the interest of others. For example, when my son Brandon's voice was changing, to avoid the embarrassment of having his voice crack in the middle of a conversation, he purposefully talked in a quiet monotone manner. Once his vocal cords matured and this cracking was no longer a problem, however, he continued to speak in a low drone.

I waited for the right time to talk to Brandon about working inflections into his speech. I gave my son a few examples of how monotone speech sounded, then helped him recall how some of his favorite people to listen to would raise and lower their voice pitch to drive home important points.

Because I had already established an "I am for you" relationship with Brandon, he was not offended. Rather, he was grateful for my suggestion. Brandon said he knew he wanted to work on being a more interesting speaker but had had no idea what changes to make.

9. Learn to Read Your Son's Body Language

Your son's body language may reveal to you how he is receiving your message, or if he is even listening to you. So observe your son's physical responses while you speak to him. If he has a glazed-over look, folded arms, or a set jaw, he may have tuned you out.

If you realize you have lost your son's attention, don't talk louder in your attempt to get him to listen. Heed the advice from Proverbs 15:1: "A soft answer turns away wrath, but a harsh word stirs up anger." If you shout, you will most likely make your son angry, not more receptive to your message. Simply make your point by talking more calmly and quietly. You will be surprised how softening your tone often reengages your listener. Then stop talking and wait for another opportunity to discuss the topic, if necessary.

10. Know When to Keep Quiet

If you want to have quality conversations with your son, learn to discern the best time to speak. Don't try to get your son to engage in a meaningful discussion when he is in front of his peers, hungry, or excessively tired.

Waiting for the best opportunity to talk to your son will allow your words to find their way into his heart, rather than get lost in a quarrel. If you, like me, experience mood swings brought on by hormonal changes, learn to hold your tongue until your levels are back to normal. The Bible says, "He who has knowledge spares his words, and a man of understanding is of a calm spirit. Even a fool is counted wise when he holds his peace; when he shuts his lips, he is considered perceptive" (Proverbs 17:27-28). When my words were influenced by mood swings, I most always played the fool. In keeping my mouth quiet, there was at least some hope that my children would consider me perceptive rather than a raving lunatic!

Even in the best of circumstances, there will be times when your words are not well received. That doesn't mean you should keep quiet to avoid *any* conflict. Although what you say may upset your son, you are still responsible for giving him direction in life. The Bible promises if you "correct your son...he will give you rest; yes, he will give delight to your soul" (Proverbs 29:17). The opposite is also true. If you ignore correcting your son, he may one day break your heart.

To ensure your words will have the greatest possible influence on your son, make sure you are walking in obedience to Christ. This discipline will make you sensitive to the Holy Spirit's leading, and that will help you to know when is the proper time to talk to your son about important issues.

11. Discern the Depths of Your Son's Thoughts

The goal of good communication is not simply to be heard, but to know your listener so you can figure out how to speak such that he will understand and apply your message. To perceive your son's deepest thoughts, carefully listen to what he is *really* saying. As he speaks, ask the Lord to give you insight into the issues your son may be contemplating.

In their book *Instructing a Child's Heart*, Tedd and Margy Tripp encourage parents to carefully understand what their child is trying to say before responding with instruction or advice: "Listening carefully to what your children are saying, and even to what they are not saying, will induce you to frame your words in ways that facilitate conversation. Without understanding, you may speak to an issue they do not even think about and may miss the things most on their minds."[2]

When you take time to search out the depths of your son's thoughts, you can encourage his right attitudes and train him from Scripture how to correct his wrong thinking. Teaching your son to ask the Lord to help him discern his own heart through the lens of Scripture will prepare him to walk in obedience to the Lord, even after he leaves your home.

12. Impart Wisdom with Kindness

Would your son describe you as a kind woman? Do you think if you are too nice your words will lose their authority? Do you rely on harsh words to get your son to respond? Or do you react defensively?

If you answer defensively, your son will not talk to you, so learn to recognize when you are becoming oversensitive. You can teach your son with kindness when you train him with the authority of God's wisdom. Proverbs 16:24 reminds us that "pleasant words are like a honeycomb, sweetness to the soul and health to the bones." The very next verse says, "There is a way that seems right to a man, but its end is the way of death" (Proverbs 16:25). Could it be that the writer of Proverbs 16 is warning us that if we insist on doing things our own way, in this case by refusing to use pleasant words, we will follow a path of destruction? Learn from the example of the Proverbs 31 mother, who "opens her mouth with wisdom, and on her tongue is the law of kindness" (Proverbs 31:26).

If you habitually speak harshly to your son, he will likely go elsewhere for advice. And if those other advisors he finds do not base their instruction in God's truth, they will likely lead your son down a road to ruin. How much better to direct your son to God's path by lovingly instructing him from Scripture!

Colossians 4:6 says, "Let your speech always be with grace, seasoned with salt, that you may know how you ought to answer each one." When your words are seasoned with grace, they will create a thirst in your son for Jesus, the Living Water.

13. Ask Forgiveness

If you tend to react emotionally to your son's infractions, your words may be sinful and unrestrained. Carelessly going on and on about an issue will do little to train your son. Proverbs 10:19 warns, "In the multitude of words sin is not lacking."

If you do react to your son in an unseemly manner, then ask him to forgive you. He will appreciate your transparency. Be sure to take responsibility for your sinful actions without turning the blame on him. "Son, I am sorry I yelled at you, but you just made me so mad" is *not* an apology, and your son will not be moved to forgive you. He will likely be put off by your blaming him for your inability to control your emotions. And your model will teach your son to likewise blame others for his wrong behavior.

When you humbly ask forgiveness, your son will learn not only how to forgive, but also to take responsibility for his own actions when he apologizes to others.

14. Get Wisdom from the Bible

Proverbs 4:5-7 says gaining wisdom should be the key pursuit in life: "Get wisdom! Get understanding!... Love her, and she will keep you. Wisdom is the principal thing; therefore get wisdom. And in all your getting, get understanding."

If you rely on the world's teachings about child rearing or ignore your responsibility to prepare yourself with biblical knowledge, your words will not carry the weight of godly wisdom, and in fact may be reckless. Proverbs 15:2 says, "The tongue of the wise uses knowledge rightly, but the mouth of fools pours forth foolishness." As you gain God's wisdom and understanding, you will be prepared to provide wise instruction to your son and direct him to the gospel of grace.

15. Remember Your Assignment

The Lord's mandate to you is to daily, deliberately, and diligently teach your son truth from God's Word. Ruth Graham, the late wife of evangelist Billy Graham, had this to say about her role as a mother: "I love being a wife, mother, and homemaker. To me it is the nicest, most rewarding job in the world, second in importance to none, not even preaching."[3]

In her lifetime, Ruth Graham's resolution to "preach" to her children and grandchildren prepared them to proclaim the gospel to the next generation. Will you share in Mrs. Graham's resolve? Will you deliberately, diligently, and daily look for opportunities to "preach" God's truth to your son?

THINKING IT THROUGH

What two virtues does Proverbs 4:7 teach us to go after? How will you pursue these virtues in your life?

LIVING IT OUT

This chapter included 15 steps for establishing better communication with your son. Write out the steps that spoke to you most and how you will apply them this week in your relationship with your son.

Watch this chapter's video teaching at
www.rhondastoppe.com/books/moms-raising-sons-to-be-men.

CHAPTER 11

THE FUTURE THAT SMILES

Don't Lose Your Focus

From the time Charles Haddon Spurgeon was 16 years old, he was a powerful preacher of the gospel. He ministered in England during the Victorian era, and the zeal that defined Spurgeon lit a fire in the people who heard his message. One of Spurgeon's contemporaries documented the influence he had on his generation:

> Did you ever walk through a village notorious for its drunkenness and profanity?...Was it ever your privilege to walk through that village again, after years, when the Gospel had been preached there? It has been mine...There went into that village a lad [Spurgeon], who had no great scholarship, but who was earnest in seeking the souls of men. He began to preach there and it pleased God to turn the whole place upside down...Where there had been robbers and villainies of every kind, all round the neighborhood, there were none, because the men who used to do the mischief

were themselves in the house of God, rejoicing to hear of Jesus crucified.[1]

Oh, for history to record such things about my son—and yours! Not accounts of earthly trophies or fame, but treasures stored up in heaven. Not how much money our sons made, but how many lives were influenced or transformed through their willing obedience to God's call on their lives. How blessed Charles's mother, Eliza Spurgeon, must have been to know God used her son to transform the generation in which he lived.

Charles Spurgeon's father, John, was an extremely busy man. He worked as a clerk in a coal merchant's office, and he also pastored a church nine miles from their home. Each Sunday he made the long journey by horse and carriage. So he was often away from home, leaving the task of bringing up the family largely to his wife, Eliza.

One Sunday while on his way to church, John Spurgeon turned the carriage around and returned home out of concern for the spiritual well-being of his four children. When he entered the house he heard the sound of earnest prayer. "He discovered," said Charles, "that it was my mother, pleading most earnestly for the salvation of all her children, and praying especially for Charles, her first-born strong-willed son. My father felt that he might safely go about his Master's business while his dear wife was caring so well for the spiritual interests of [the children]."[2]

Charles looked back on his mother with deep affection and gratitude. He told of her reading Scripture to her children and pleading with them to be concerned about their souls. "I cannot tell how much I owe to the solemn words of my good mother," he wrote. "I remember on one occasion her praying thus, 'Now, Lord, if my children go on in their sins, it will not be from ignorance that they perish...' How can I ever forget when she bowed her knee, and with her arms about my neck, prayed, 'Oh, that my son may live before Thee!'"[3]

Oh, how priceless for Eliza's son to attribute the beginning of all the greatness and goodness of her children to her, by God's grace. Wouldn't you be blessed beyond measure to hear your son say such words about you?

Only God knows fully the powerful influence Eliza Spurgeon's devotion to Scripture and prayer had upon her children. Charles learned the importance of prayer from her, and he in turn taught his congregation to pray. When asked, "To what do you attribute your success?" Spurgeon answered, "My people pray for me."[4]

Eliza Spurgeon's devotion to Christ not only inspired her children to live godly lives, but also an entire generation of people was ignited with passion for prayer and the spreading of the gospel through her Christ-centered influence.

God Can Use the "Untrained"

Spurgeon was an amazing preacher who did not have a college education. Although he lacked the college degree most churches expected of their ministers in his era, Spurgeon was well prepared for ministry through his constant and passionate study of Scripture.

In 1854, after inviting Spurgeon to speak for a few Sundays to the congregation, the deacons of New Park Street Chapel in London called Spurgeon to be their pastor. He was 19 years old at the time, and evidently they didn't view his lack of a college degree as a liability. This was somewhat surprising considering that several of the church's earlier pastors had been well-known and highly regarded Bible teachers and the church was among London's most prominent and historic Baptist churches. The deacons agreed that Spurgeon's preaching was filled with the passion they were looking for. As it turned out, his unique style of preaching would have a remarkable influence upon London for the next 38 years, until his death in 1892.

And today, God continues to use those who, from a human standpoint, are "untrained." From His perspective, they are instruments ready for use. My husband, Steve, has two young men right now who are his associate pastors in our church. Dale is our youth pastor, and Nathan is our worship pastor. Their zeal for the gospel and love of Scripture remind me of Spurgeon. Like Spurgeon, neither one has a formal education in biblical studies. But for the past two decades both have been taught, mentored, and trained how to study the Bible, preach, and do the work of the ministry. Their willing service to the Lord has blessed my husband, our church, and our community beyond measure.

Both Dale and Nathan grew up in Christian homes, through which the Lord sovereignly laid a godly foundation in each of their lives. Both attended public high schools and had many friends who did not know Christ. This compelled Dale and Nathan to share the gospel with teens.

Nathan says, "My mother instilled in us the importance of knowing who Christ is, and sharing that with everyone. We were taught that school was a place where *everyone* was."

Nathan's mother, Christina, also saw herself as a "missionary" on public school campuses. Although Christina did not learn to read well until later in life, she refused to resign herself to the insecurities caused by her academic challenges and became very involved on the campuses of her children. Christina even served on the school board.

When Christina's youngest son, Daniel, graduated from high school, his deep concern for his friends to know Christ was evident by the fact he used his salutatorian speech to deliver a powerful gospel message—first in English, then in Spanish!

Do you consider yourself or your son too average to do anything momentous for God? Do either of you have physical or academic impediments that have made you insecure about serving the Lord? Be encouraged—God delights in using ordinary lives to do great things for His kingdom. If your son is a Christian, he has been made alive in Christ to accomplish kingdom purposes! Helping your son to see himself through his wonderful identity in Christ will train him to anticipate the future the Lord has planned for him.

Ephesians 2:10 teaches that before time began, God prepared good works for His followers to fulfill during their time upon the earth.

Contemplate these amazing truths: The God of all creation knows your son's name, ordained the age in which he would live, and wants to do good works through him to accomplish "His good pleasure" (Philippians 2:13). Do you believe God can achieve His purposes through your son? When you talk to your son about his future, do you teach him with confidence that God does extraordinary works through anyone who is willing to serve Him? Do you remind your son that God wants to use his obedient life today, and every day afterward? Not somewhere down the road, but now!

Be encouraged—God delights in using ordinary lives to do great things for His kingdom.

God's Word reveals many examples of how He leads His servants. King David made it clear the Lord is intimately involved in our lives. In Psalm 139 he wrote, "You have hedged me behind and before, and laid Your hand upon me. Such knowledge is too wonderful for me... Where can I go from Your Spirit?... Your hand shall lead me" (verses 5-7, 10).

If your son is not a Christian, the best witnessing tool you have for winning him to Christ is your own life of joyful service to the Lord. Be ever mindful that your son is observing how you live to see if your relationship with Jesus makes a difference. Religious duty will not draw your son to your Savior; rather, your wholehearted surrender to the One you call Lord will speak volumes to him as he tries to decide whether he needs or wants a relationship with Jesus. If your desire is to draw your son to Christ, your foremost goals should be to live the gospel message through your conversations and actions and pray for God to draw your son to Jesus.

So how can you equip your son for a future of service that brings glory to God? That brings us to our next principle for raising up a son to be a godly man.

PRINCIPLE 6: Teach Your Son to Think Biblically

———

What does it mean to think biblically? Simply stated, it means to filter all of life's experiences through God's Word. To instill a scriptural foundation in your son, you will need to know the Bible well enough to season your conversations with sound doctrine. God said, "My people are destroyed for lack of knowledge" (Hosea 4:6). So to keep your son from being destroyed by worldly influences and deception, impart knowledge from the Bible as often as the opportunity arises.

Concerning preparing ourselves with Scripture to effectively lead others to grow in their faith, D.L. Moody, a prominent evangelist and minister of the nineteenth century, said, "If we attempt to feed others we must first be fed ourselves."[5] Steve Miller, author of *D.L. Moody on Spiritual Leadership*, explains: "When we take the time to ensure our lives abound with spiritual water, [the people we lead] are more likely to abound with spiritual fruit."[6]

In Deuteronomy 6:4-9, a key parenting passage, you'll find a simple outline for how to develop a biblical worldview in your son's mind:

1. You must love the Lord your God with all your heart, with all your soul, and with all your strength. Your wholehearted commitment to God and His Word will demonstrate to your son how much you love God and value Scripture.

2. Think about, meditate on, and memorize God's Word so that your obedience to God will be a response based upon biblical precepts. When you transform your thinking with God's Word, you will be prepared to teach your son how to speak and act in God-honoring ways. You'll also be equipped to train your son to think biblically.

3. Relate your son's everyday experiences to the Bible. This practice will make talking about spiritual matters a normal part of your conversations with your son.

The world would instruct your son to achieve all of his goals for his own pleasure and fame, rather than for God's glory. That is why it is vital for you to train him to filter his opportunities and achievements through a biblical mindset.

As you commit to teaching your son to think biblically, regularly remind him that God wants to use him to draw others to Christ. The talents and abilities you observe in your son will be used for their greatest good when he learns to live with a passion for the cross of Christ. In 1 Corinthians 2:1-5, the apostle Paul describes the characteristics of a person focused completely on the life-changing reality of the gospel:

> I, brethren, when I came to you, did not come with excellence of speech or of wisdom declaring to you the testimony of God. For I determined not to know anything among you except Jesus Christ and Him crucified. I was with you in weakness, in fear, and in much trembling. And my speech and my preaching were not with persuasive words of human wisdom, but in demonstration of the Spirit and of power, that your faith should not be in the wisdom of men but in the power of God.

This passage reveals Paul's central point. He did not want to distract from the critical message of salvation with a multitude of words about other topics. In this cultural climate, it can be tempting to get so riled up about the injustices, political differences, or personal preferences that your passion for Christ gets drowned out. While it is important to stand for what is right, follow the apostle Paul's example by choosing to preach the gospel of salvation to a world that is lost without a Savior. Paul preached Christ at a time when Nero was burning Rome and blaming Christians. Paul himself was tormented unjustly because of his message, but he never wavered from his purpose of making Christ known.

Paul's letters did not contain rants about the tyrant who was persecuting Christians. Rather, Paul continually asked, "[Pray] also for us, that God would open to us a door for the word, to speak the mystery of Christ, for which I am also in chains" (Colossians 4:3). The apostle knew what the death, burial, and resurrection of Christ had meant to him. And Paul clearly understood that the only hope *anyone* has lies in the cross of Christ. The real need for our world is not political intervention, but repentance and salvation.

When you teach your son about salvation, do you tremble under the weight of the significance of this message? Do you shudder to think about who you would be without Christ? I am painfully aware of how wretched I am without my Savior. So that you do not forget who you would be without Christ, establish a habit of rehearsing to yourself and your son how the gospel has transformed your life. Remind yourself frequently of how God saved you, and like the apostle Paul, don't ever tire of talking about the miraculous life Jesus gives to those who receive Him as Savior.

The incredible truth that God makes us alive in Christ simply because of His rich mercy, great love, amazing grace, and tremendous kindness makes me want to shout, "Hallelujah!" I pray you never take for granted the miracle of salvation. May you always be amazed at the supernatural event that occurs when one is raised from dead in their sins to be made alive in Christ.

Don't Lose Your Focus

Life is filled with distractions. Football practice, homework, and social events are not in and of themselves bad things. But if they become your focal points, you will undoubtedly direct your attention (and your son's attention) to whatever pursuit has priority at the moment. Remember that each activity is an avenue for you, and your son, to let your light shine to people who are lost and in need of a Savior. Learn to pray throughout your day, and you will be ever mindful of conducting yourself in a way that brings glory to God.

Take time to share with your son the way God used teenagers in the Bible to accomplish His purposes. This will inspire him to look forward to however God might work through his young life to influence his generation as well. In chapter 1 of this book, we talked about King David's courage. Let's revisit David's story and look for ways you could teach your son how God works in the lives of young men.

First Samuel 17 records the incredible story of David killing the giant Goliath. David was a teenager when he went to the battlefield to deliver supplies to his three older brothers. There, he found his brothers—and the army of Israel—hiding from the Philistine army. When David learned that for 40 days Goliath had been mocking the Israelite army and challenging them to send a warrior to fight him, he declared he would do battle against the giant.

What happened when David stepped forth with great courage?

1. David's motives were questioned.

When David said he would fight Goliath, his oldest brother, Eliab, challenged David's intentions and called him prideful. But Eliab's misinterpretation of his younger brother's motives did not sway David's resolve. David simply said, "Is there not a cause?" (1 Samuel 17:29).

There is something about a cause that ignites a fire in the hearts of teenagers. And when it is the cause of God, godly teens will go to great lengths—even to the point of sacrificing their own lives—for the Lord's purposes.

If your son steps up to do something courageous, be prepared for his peers to question his motives. Help your son learn how to search his own heart and pray that his motives are God-honoring. And teach him that when he knows God will be pleased with his actions, he does not need to worry about what ungodly people think.

2. David was told he was too young.

When King Saul saw how young David was, he immediately discounted David's ability to fight the giant. After all, Goliath had many years of experience as a warrior. David did not become discouraged by Saul's lack of faith in his abilities because David's faith rested in God. David recounted to Saul how, as a young shepherd boy, the Lord had enabled him to kill a lion and a bear with his bare hands so he could protect his father's sheep.

When your son's abilities are questioned because he is young, remind him that if he is serving the Lord, he should "let no one despise [his] youth" (1 Timothy 4:12). To help your son not grow disheartened when he faces a difficult challenge, remind him of how God allowed the lion and bear attacks so David could grow in his faith. As your son recalls how God worked to make David a courageous warrior for the Lord, he will learn to recognize God's hand amid his own struggles and find the strength to trust the Lord.

Are there lions and bears in your son's life? Can you learn to trust the Lord's sovereignty over what He allows your son to endure? Sometimes we moms are so busy rescuing our sons from trials that we get in the way of how God is working to build their faith. In the future, God may ask your son to fight a giant. Will you allow the Lord to prepare your son for the battle?

3. The odds were against David.

King Saul tried to suit David with his armor, but it was too big and heavy and encumbered David's walk. And though Goliath was a hardened warrior with an iron spearhead that weighed 15 pounds, David chose to do battle with nothing more than a slingshot and five small stones.

There will be times when your son faces challenges that seem too big for him. The world will throw their ideas of "weapons for success" at your son. But you can teach your son that, just like David's sling and stones, God can help bring victory through unexpected resources. He will provide your son with the means for facing a challenge in the very moment he needs them.

4. God was with David.

King Saul said, "Go, and the Lord be with you!" (1 Samuel 17:37). David's confidence that the Lord was with him became evident to all when he proclaimed to Goliath, "I come to you in the name of the LORD of hosts, the God of the armies of Israel, whom you have defied" (1 Samuel 17:45). To equip your son to be courageous when he thinks he stands alone, encourage him to memorize 1 John 4:4: "He who is in you is greater than he who is in the world." When you remind your son that the Spirit of the living God dwells in his heart to give him strength and courage, you prepare him to accomplish whatever it is the Lord asks him to do.

5. David had faith.

When David was face-to-face with the giant on the battlefield, he did not waver in his resolve. Rather, he said to Goliath, "This day the LORD will deliver you into my hand, and I will strike you and take your head from you" (1 Samuel 17:46).

David did not look at his unnerving circumstances and cower under pressure. Rather, he looked right at his enemy and, in belief, proclaimed conquest. In the same way, there will be times when your son will have to courageously step out to do God's work. One of the best ways to teach your son how to live by faith is to demonstrate confidence in God yourself. Let your son observe, in your life, how true faith is lived out every day.

6. David had a proper perspective.

David's goal was not to make a name for himself, but to glorify God. His righteous courage came from a deep longing to defend the name of the God of Israel. First Samuel 17:46 clearly defines

David's purpose in fighting the giant: "that all the earth may know that there is a God in Israel."

From David's example, you can teach your son what it means to glorify God. David's desire was not to draw attention to himself, but to uphold God's glory. Because David clearly understood the purpose of his mission, he knew who would help him emerge victoriously. His desire was for all who were watching that day—and for all who would hear the account of this notorious battle—to honor the Lord.

David was a shepherd boy who was also a musician and poet. He was a skilled archer and warrior as well. By teaching your son about the life of David, you can help him discover that David was involved in many activities, and he did each of them to the best of his ability. Because David's accomplishments were never about his own fame, but rather about exalting the name of God, the Lord gave him great success.

Heroes of the Faith

In the Bible, there are other teenagers through whom God accomplished great feats. You can tell your son about Joseph, Samuel, Daniel, Shadrach, Meshach, and Abed-Nego. Helping your son discover how each young man devoted his life to serving the Lord can plant a seed in his heart to commit his future to God as well. And when you teach your son how those same men are now reaping eternal rewards from their service to God, you will inspire him to live with an eternal perspective.

You can also introduce your son to the "heroes of the faith" listed in Hebrews chapter 11. Immediately after reading about these heroes we are told, "Since we are surrounded by so great a cloud of witnesses, let us lay aside every weight, and the sin which so easily ensnares us, and let us run with endurance the race that is set before us, looking unto Jesus, the author and finisher of our faith" (Hebrews 12:1-2).

Teaching your son about Bible heroes will inspire him to live like them. Will you run the race with heroic faith? Your example will earn you the privilege of asking your son to grasp the baton you are handing him…so that he can continue this great relay race of Christian heroes through the ages.

THINKING IT THROUGH

Write out Proverbs 16:9. What can you learn about God's sovereignty from this verse? How will understanding God's sovereignty influence the way you teach your son about his future?

Proverbs 16:3 says, "Commit your works to the LORD, and your thoughts will be established." In your own words, explain one way you can teach your son to commit his works to the Lord.

LIVING IT OUT

Write the commands that appear in Hebrews 12:1-2. How can

obeying these commands help you and your son to "run with endurance the race that is set before us"?

Watch this chapter's video teaching at
www.rhondastoppe.com/books/moms-raising-sons-to-be-men.

CHAPTER 12

YOU *CAN* DO THIS

The Key to Success

When I was growing up, each morning my father would put on a pot of coffee, go for a jog, and return to our living room to pray. When I woke up and staggered toward the kitchen for my breakfast, I would smell the coffee and, in the living room, see my father in his jogging attire, on his knees in prayer. I cannot begin to tell you the security that washed over me each morning when I saw my dad interceding before the Lord. To this day, there are times when the smell of early morning coffee brings back the peaceful feelings I experienced as a child when I saw my father praying. (Maybe that's why I love coffee so much!)

In the same way, if your son observes you praying, he will gain a quiet confidence from knowing that his mother is going to the very throne of God for strength and wisdom to face the day. And as you continue in communion with the Lord, your relationship with Him will grow deeper and your faith will grow stronger. It has been said, "No prayer, no power; much prayer, much power." I am convinced that prayer is essential to becoming the mother your heart longs to be. I echo the apostle Paul's prayer for you: "Therefore [I] also pray always for you that our God would count you worthy of this calling, and fulfill all the good pleasure of His goodness and the work of faith with power, that the name of our Lord Jesus Christ may be glorified in you, and you in Him, according to the grace of our God and the Lord Jesus Christ" (2 Thessalonians 1:11-12).

What Is Success?

Your success as a mother does not depend upon what your son chooses to do with his life. Rather, according to Scripture, success lies in *your* obedience to God—in what *you* choose to do with your life. If you get nothing else out of this book, get this:

> If your son observes you praying, he will gain a quiet confidence from knowing that his mother is going to the very throne of God for strength and wisdom to face the day.

God has called you to the ministry of motherhood. And with that calling He has provided the Holy Spirit to lead you and guide you in your journey. By committing to know God through His Word, you will grow to love Him more each day, and when you love God properly, you will love your son correctly. The Lord has provided tools for you to do well in your calling. By daily communing with Him through the Bible, prayer, worship, and fellowship with the church, you will be fully equipped for this incredible privilege of bringing up your son, because God will work through you to raise your son for His glory.

With that in mind, let's look at one final principle for raising your son to be a godly man:

PRINCIPLE 7: God Is Your Source of Wisdom and Strength

––––––

Prayer is an avenue for you to obtain strength from the Lord. James 5:16 promises, "The effective, fervent prayer of a righteous [person] avails much." In the 18 years that my husband was in youth ministry, we learned no matter how different the parenting styles of the parents of the teens in our youth ministry, the students who had Christian parents praying for them were by far the most grounded in their faith. In this age of always *doing* something, prayer can seem like a waste of time. But I believe prayer is the most neglected resource that parents have at their disposal.

Sadly, for many of us, prayer is an afterthought. When it comes to seeking a solution for a situation, after all other avenues have been exhausted, how often have you heard someone say, "All we can do now is pray"? Learn to make prayer your first, central, *and* last resort. Or else, in all your doing, if there is no praying, your best efforts will be in vain.

When Jesus taught His disciples to pray, He began, "*When* you pray" (Matthew 6:5). Notice He said *when*, not *if*. Jesus's word choice presupposes that His disciples will be characterized by prayer. Would your son say that prayer characterizes your life?

The Power of Your Prayers

In Scripture, we read about Hannah, who prayed for the Lord to give her a son. She vowed that if God granted her request, she would bring her son to the temple to serve God all of his days. In 1 Samuel 1:10–2:11, you can read about how God answered Hannah's prayer. One Bible teacher says this about this mother who was a prayer warrior: "Hannah is a reminder that mothers are the makers of men and the architects of the next generation. Her earnest prayer for a child was the beginning of a series of events that helped turn back the spiritual darkness and backsliding in Israel. She set in motion a chain of events that would ultimately usher in a profound spiritual awakening at the dawn of the Davidic dynasty."[1]

Have you ever considered mothers as architects of the next

generation? Or that your prayers could set in motion a chain of events for a spiritual awakening? It's no wonder Satan tries to keep us too busy to pray.

Your Adequacy Is from God

Every woman who has raised sons for God's glory has found her effectiveness not in her own abilities, but in her relationship with the Lord. Second Corinthians 3:5 reminds us that only God can make us adequate to do His work. For the ministry of motherhood, the Lord has given you everything you need for life and godliness in Christ Jesus (2 Peter 1:3). And He has given you His treasured resource, the Bible, to direct you because "it gives understanding to the simple" (Psalm 119:130).

As a young mother, I learned the important principle of studying Scripture. With each hour I spend in Bible study, God changes me into a woman, wife, and mother I never would have been without His transforming power. And He can do the same for you. It's simply not possible for you to be a godly mother if you forsake the tools God has given to make you adequate for His work. To raise a godly son does not require you to know everything about the Bible. All that God asks is that you determine to always be learning more, and to *live what you do know*.

Be Strong and Courageous

The best advice I can give any mother who would seek to lead her son to live for the Lord is the words God spoke to Joshua when he became Israel's leader after Moses's death:

> Be strong and very courageous, that you may observe to do according to all the law…Do not turn from it to the right hand or to the left, that you may prosper wherever you go. This Book of the Law shall not depart from your mouth, but you shall meditate in it day and night,

that you may observe to do according to all that is written in it. For then you will make your way prosperous,
and then you will have good success. Have I not commanded you? Be strong and of good courage; do not be
afraid, nor be dismayed, for the LORD your God is with
you wherever you go (Joshua 1:7-9).

Can you imagine how Joshua must have felt as the new leader
of Israel? His mentor, Moses, had died. Besides having to deal with
the grief of losing the man he had loved dearly and served under
for decades, Joshua now faced the daunting task of leading Israel
into battle against all their enemies. If you have ever felt even a bit
of what Joshua must have felt, you can envision how refreshing and
energizing God's words would have been for Joshua. Will you allow
God's words to revive you as well? As you purpose to lead your son
to victory in his own battles to live a God-honoring life, will you
take to heart God's advice to Joshua? Meditate on His Word day and
night, and do all that He commands, and you will succeed.

Let Christ Invade Your Life

Your son's generation longs to see what genuine Christianity
looks like. They are aching for someone to lay down all the trivial
cares of life and show them, by example, what it really means to live
for Christ. Your son can come to understand the infinite importance of surrendering his future to the Lord if he sees you living
with total abandon for the Lord. And through your example, your
son can learn to joyfully expect the Lord to direct his future as well.

When Christ invades your life, what spills over is a passion for
Him and for His kingdom purposes. Your son will not be able to
ignore your message if it flows from a genuine longing to honor the
Lord in all you do.

To let Christ invade your life, you may need to do a little house-
cleaning. To determine whether you are serious about living in a

manner that will inspire your son to live for Christ, ask yourself these questions:

- Am I willing to forfeit relationships that do not honor the Lord?

- Am I willing to refuse to be entertained by anything that is contrary to God's commands?

- Am I willing to forsake all activities or opportunities that would draw me away from wholehearted obedience to Christ?

Your willingness to lay aside anything that besets your passionate pursuit of Christ and His leading not only will set an example for your son to follow, but also will create an appetite in him to do the same. To make a lasting impression on your son, you must be set on fire by the single most glorious purpose of life—to know Christ and joyfully exhibit His greatness in *all* areas of life!

How Can I Change?

As you have read through this book, has the Lord shown you areas in your life that He would like to shape so that you are more like Christ? Are you wondering, *How can I change? How can I help my son to change?*

True change will not come by simply resolving to do better. Even if you determine to work harder to be a better parent, know this about change: Although you may be able to amend your actions, if there is not an inward heart change brought about by the Lord's work, your adjustments will be made in your own feeble power and not God's divine enabling power. So daily seek to allow God to mold you more to the image of Christ by walking closely to Him through Bible study, prayer, and fellowship with other believers. It is only as the heart truly changes that real-life changes take place. And the process of change is slow, so don't get discouraged. When you fall back into sinful habits, don't give up. Repent and align yourself with what God desires for your life.

As you pursue biblical change, the Lord will faithfully help you put to death old sinful habits and take on new God-honoring obedient ways. And when those changes joyfully reflect Christ to your son, the transformation he sees in you will speak more to him about your faith than any words you can say.

Will you draw near to the Lord through repentance, prayer, God's Word, fellowship with believers, and godly mentors? For through these you will be empowered by the Spirit of the Living God with strength and wisdom to fulfill the purpose God has ordained for you. And you will become the mom you always hoped you would be—a mother without regrets.

THINKING IT THROUGH

Psalm 145:4 says, "One generation shall praise Your works to another, and shall declare Your mighty acts." Name some ways you can praise the Lord and declare His mighty acts to your son. Will you commit yourself to making a habit of praising God's works before your son?

LIVING IT OUT

One of the best ways to live out what you've learned is to teach it to someone else. God's plan is for you and me to mentor mothers.

Please consider going back through this book with a friend. Or, even better, create a small group study (in person or online) to walk through these pages together.

Now, write a prayer of commitment to the Lord, asking Him to help you as you teach your son to know Him through your life example. May your example guide your son toward a life without regrets.

Finally, let's take some time to review the seven principles for raising godly sons that we have covered in Part 2 of this book:

Principle 1: Teaching your son to respect authority prepares him to respect God's authority.

Principle 2: Have a clear idea of the kind of man God calls your son to be.

Principle 3: Guide your son toward independence.

Principle 4: Knowing your son well allows you to encourage his strengths and correct his weaknesses.

Principle 5: Talk so your son listens, and listen so he talks.

Principle 6: Teach your son to think biblically.

Principle 7: God is your source of wisdom and strength.

Watch this chapter's video teaching at
www.rhondastoppe.com/books/moms-raising-sons-to-be-men.

PART THREE

EVEN IF...

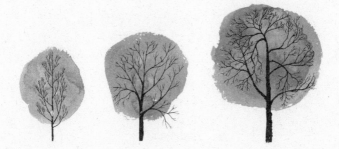

CHAPTER 13

EVEN IF HE WANDERS

Hope for the Prodigal

One of my favorite words of encouragement to share with mothers of prodigals is when Jesus revealed to Peter: "Satan has asked for you, that he may sift you as wheat" (Luke 22:31). Jesus didn't leave His disciple with that horror hanging over his head though. Jesus encouraged Peter by saying, "But I have prayed for you" (verse 32).

Let this wash over you: Our Savior intercedes for us and our children. Even when the enemy tries to interfere with His plan for their lives, Jesus prays for them.

Hebrews 7:25 promises that Jesus "always lives to make intercession for them." Oh what a blessing to know our Savior is praying for our sons. Even when the enemy tries to steal, kill, and destroy, it is God who works in them "to will and to do for His good pleasure" (Philippians 2:13).

PKs Can Be Okay

As a pastor's wife, raising children in the fishbowl of ministry was always a concern. If you're a pastor's wife, you understand the pressures of being a pastor's kid—a "PK." I trembled under the weight of my responsibility. But my goal was not to raise my children so that the church would think well of their daddy. Rather, my desire was to raise them to love and follow Jesus, no matter what their daddy did for a living.

One day, Brandon learned that one of his friends was suffering from a drug addiction and had been kicked out of his home. Brandon went to Steve and told him what had happened. And then he said, "Dad, my friend's parents sent him away because he's using cocaine. Would you send me away if I started using drugs?"

Steve pondered a moment. Then he replied, "Son, if you were using drugs, I would quit my job as a pastor, strap on my nail bags, and go back to work in construction. I'd take you with me every day and not leave your side."

Junior-high Brandon attempted to hold back his tears. But as they began to fall, he hugged his father and said, "Thanks, Dad."

Brandon never tested Steve's promise. But it meant the world to our son that his father would choose his ministry to Brandon over his ministry to the church.

On another occasion, Brandon complained, "If Dad weren't a pastor, you'd let me go skateboarding around town."

My response? "Dude, if your dad was still swinging a hammer, we wouldn't let you skate all over town unsupervised." The town where my husband pastors is known for meth addiction. And many young boys have been seduced into this horrible addiction by naïvely being in the wrong place at the wrong time without supervision.

Still, I was glad Brandon put into words the idea that had been rolling around in his head. We never wanted our kids to think we made parenting decisions because of their dad's job. So when moody, adolescent Brandon spoke his mind, it was an opportunity to right his wrong thinking.

As a side note, during his hormonally imbalanced adolescent

years, I remember telling Brandon, "Son, don't ever smoke a joint. Because I guarantee you're gonna like how it makes you feel. But the highs and lows you're feeling as an adolescent are part of growing into a mature man. And if you self-medicate with pot, you're not going to learn how to manage your emotions."

I then went on to remind him of a person we knew who had little control over his angry outbursts. This person had used marijuana since he was a teen. He was married and with children when he finally stopped using. Unfortunately, the anger he had suppressed with drugs for two decades was out of control because he had never learned how to manage it.

I remember pondering if I should even bring up marijuana when Brandon was in a mood. I recall thinking, *I don't want to put the idea in his head.* But then I remembered how the apostle Paul cautioned, "Lest Satan should take advantage of us; for we are not ignorant of his devices" (2 Corinthians 2:11). Momma, sometimes it may feel like it's better to leave things unsaid, but follow the example of the apostle Paul by making the most of opportunities to help your son be aware of Satan's schemes.

So what hope does a mother have if her child rebels? Do not lose heart. Many men whom God has used to accomplish astounding feats for the kingdom rebelled against their Christian upbringing for a time. Their moms did not give up on them, and neither did the Lord. In fact, He pursued them with divine foresight and intervention to bring each one to repentance. And when they returned, there was no stopping their passionate obedience to God's calling.

Adoniram Judson was a pastor's kid—another "PK." His father was a Puritan preacher. When Adoniram left his home in Rhode Island for Brown University, all that he knew about God was challenged. Adoniram's faith waned, and eventually he denounced it altogether as he sat under the teachings of atheistic professors and became close friends with Jacob Eames—who laughed loudest at the idea of a personal God, a literal devil, or the existence of heaven and hell.

After Adoniram graduated from Brown, he went to New York to pursue a career as a playwright and actor. But he found that all he had learned at the university had done little to prepare him for life in the real world.

Worn-out and dejected, Adoniram wandered farther away from home. One night through God's providence, he happened upon a roadside inn with just one room available for the night. However, the innkeeper warned him that the man in the next room was dying in excruciating pain. Adoniram's hardened heart was certain that the man's death would not faze him, and he fully expected to sleep soundly.

Throughout the night, Adoniram could hear the man's cries of agony. Adoniram was surprised how thoughts he had long dismissed kept going through his mind:

What will happen to this man's soul on the other side of death? And even more chilling, *What would I be facing tonight if I were dying instead of him?*

The next morning, the innkeeper told Adoniram the young man had died during the night. For some reason, Adoniram asked for the name of the deceased man. "Jacob Eames," responded the innkeeper. The very classmate of Adoniram who had mocked the idea of God's existence!

The news sent Adoniram home, looking for answers. The Lord used the death of his friend to bring Adoniram to his spiritual senses. Adoniram enrolled in seminary that year, and eventually he became the first American missionary on foreign soil. He translated the entire Bible into the Burmese language, and he led more than 7,000 people to Christ in India before his death in 1850.

For over a decade, whenever I've shared Adoniram Judson's story at a speaking engagement, I watch the tears fall from mothers' eyes. Some are amid a son's or daughter's rebellion, and others have young children but are tenderhearted, realizing how often Satan attempts to sift our children like wheat.

As a parent, you'll come to see that there are times when children fall into sin and rebel against God. They may refuse to turn from their sinful ways and reject their parents' guidance and God's authority over their lives. What should you do if you find yourself in that situation? A story Jesus tells in Luke 15:11-32 teaches us how to respond.

When the younger son in that story asked his father to give him his inheritance early, his father acquiesced. The young prodigal left home and squandered every penny of his father's money on careless, unholy living. It's important to observe that even though the son's choices would cost him dearly, the father never ran after him. Instead, the brokenhearted father stayed home and watched the horizon with the hope that one day, his rebellious son would return.

Notice also that the father allowed his son to experience the consequences of his foolishness. Rather than sending his son more money after the inheritance was squandered, the father let his son suffer from his rebellious choices. The father did not attempt to rescue, manipulate, or "guilt" the son into returning home. He simply waited for God to do whatever was necessary to bring his son to repentance. And then, when the son returned, the father welcomed him with open arms.

As much as you may ache over your son's rebellion, remember that only the Lord can arrange circumstances to break your son's hard heart (2 Samuel 14:14). Your attempt to control or engineer your son's contrition may serve to push him further away, or it may get in the way of whatever lessons God is trying to teach your son.

One of the worst things you can do is try to rescue your son from the consequences of his rebellion. God is likely working to bring him to brokenness, and your intervention may delay the Lord's work. The greatest influence you can have upon a prodigal son is faithful prayer for his repentance from sin.

Even as I am writing this chapter, I can joyfully celebrate how, ten years ago, my nephew Adrian returned from his prodigal ways.

He is now a godly husband and father raising his children to know the Lord. For years I watched his parents follow the example from the Bible by praying for Adrian and refusing to rescue him from his destructive choices. Adrian's return to the Lord is evidence of the power of prayer!

Saint Augustine's Mom

Aurelius Augustine, who was born in AD 354, was a prodigal. His sinful rebellion grieved his mother. "Yet through it all, one thing remained constant: Aurelius had a godly, praying mother named Monica. He had broken her heart as a rebellious youth, but not her love. He had soiled her name, but nothing could stop her prayers."[1]

Augustine's mother once asked a bishop to talk to her son. The bishop replied, "No...pray to the Lord that he will discover *by reading* what his error is." Seeing her devout commitment to praying for her son's repentance, the bishop "looked deeply into Monica's weeping eyes and said: But be sure of this...It is impossible that the son of these tears should perish."[2]

After many years of perverted and riotous living, the Lord penetrated Augustine's hardened heart by orchestrating circumstances in which he read Romans 13:14: "Put on the Lord Jesus Christ, and make no provision for the flesh, to fulfill its lusts." In an instant, Augustine understood that Jesus was his only answer. When he received Christ as Savior, his mother danced with joy. In his *Confessions*, Augustine wrote, "Thou didst call, and cry, and burst my deafness. Thou didst gleam, and glow, and dispel my blindness. Thou didst touch me, and I burned for thy peace."[3]

Augustine spent the remaining 40 years of his life defending the doctrines of the Christian church. God answered the determined prayers of his godly mother and brought a change of heart to a man who went on to set the tone for Western Christian theology and thought for centuries.

God is the only One who can draw the prodigal to Himself, but you can have a tremendous influence through your quiet and consistent intercession. Will you determine to faithfully pray for your son? Don't ever give up!

If you have a son who has departed from his godly roots, I hope Adoniram Judson's story will give you the courage to trust the Lord. And if your son is in rebellion against God, rather than shamefully hiding your burden, enlist the prayer support of other godly mothers. Satan loves secrets and shame. When the first signs of defiance begin to show in your son, Satan will tell you to keep it to yourself because of what others will think of you. But this is precisely when you must *make yourself vulnerable* and ask others to pray. Do not allow your pride to keep you from requesting prayer, or cause you to wait to ask for prayer until your son has wandered so far from the faith that his heart has hardened.

When you know you have made mistakes in raising your son, it's possible for your remorse to keep you from asking for support. After all, it's easy to find people who will pass judgment and point out what you did wrong. But don't go to them for help. Find a few strong Christian friends whom you can trust. Ask them for godly counsel, and then join with them in praying for your son's repentance. Consistent, committed prayer will do more to draw your son back to Christ than any other action you can take.

Jeanne Hendricks, wife of Dallas Theological Seminary professor Howard Hendricks, said one of the most traumatic times of her life was when their adolescent son went through a period of rebellion. Jeanne said, "He was so far from the Lord and from us. I felt like the devil himself was out to get my child. I prayed as I never prayed before." For the season of her son's rebellion, Jeanne fasted each day's noon meal and prayed until God broke through to him.

Jeanne has prayed her family through more than a few hardships. Listen to what she says about those times: "It is as if the heavenly Father has said, *I love you so much that I must allow you to be hurt sometimes to help you see Me as I really am, to experience My comfort,*

My steady hand, My voice in the storm. I am convinced that no other curriculum could teach God's lovingkindness more effectively than that of mothering."[4]

If your son goes through a season that breaks your heart, learn from Jeanne's example and pray him through it. Remember, there are many godly men who at one time were rebellious yet went on to accomplish great feats for the Lord's kingdom. "Our God is the God of salvation; and to GOD the Lord belong escapes from death" (Psalm 68:20).

THINKING IT THROUGH

Second Samuel 14:14 says that God "devises means, so that His banished ones are not expelled from Him." Consider how God devised the means for Adoniram Judson to come upon his dying friend. How does this story bring hope to the parent of a prodigal?

LIVING IT OUT

Raising kids in church, teaching them about Jesus, and showing them the way to salvation are essential. If you're a parent of a prodigal, you know how Satan can seduce a child away. Find courage in remembering that Jesus prays for your prodigal. And I do too. Right here and right now—

Lord Jesus, please devise a way to bring this prodigal child to repentance and true salvation. Amen!

Take time to consider how God might use you to encourage a

parent of a prodigal. Determine to pray for their child, and let the parent know you're praying.

Watch this chapter's video teaching at
www.rhondastoppe.com/books/moms-raising-sons-to-be-men.

CHAPTER 14

EVEN IF YOU DON'T KNOW WHAT TO SAY

How to Talk to Your Son about Sex and Purity

When your adolescent son begins to show interest in a girl, it's tempting to simply say, "No. You're too young to have those feelings." But this is one instance when the "because I said so" response will likely do more harm than good.

I can remember when our youngest daughter had become attracted to Estevan, her brother's best friend. Since Estevan's mother had passed away, I knew he was not hearing any godly counsel about how he could express his feelings for Kayla in a biblical manner. Steve and I asked Kayla and Estevan not to date for the time being.

One day Estevan mentioned to me that he wanted to learn to drive a car with a stick shift. I happened to have an old model BMW with four-on-the-floor, so I offered to teach him how to drive my car. It was a beautiful spring day, and since the car was a convertible, it seemed a perfect day to take a drive. I handed my keys to Estevan and said, "Let's go."

Kayla joined us in the back seat. As we drove and Estevan got the hang of shifting while using the clutch, we began a lighthearted visit. Then Estevan turned to me and said, "Why does Steve hate me?"

Poor boy. He was still trying to process why Steve wouldn't let Kayla be his girlfriend. On several occasions, Estevan had invited Kayla to come to his house after school to hang out. Steve always said no.

I looked into Estevan's eyes and said, "Estevan, Steve loves you a lot. He loves Kayla too. He sees that the two of you deeply care for each other. The problem is you are both so young. Maybe God will allow you to marry each other one day, but that will be a long way off. Steve's desire is to help you and Kayla discern God's will in what He would have for your relationship. And Steve and I both know that if we allow you to spend time alone as a couple, the odds are you won't remain sexually pure over the many years you will have to wait to be married, if that's what God has for the two of you."

Kayla's eyes got as big as saucers as I went on. "It's not just about not having sex until you're married. It's about remaining pure so God can lead each of you by His Spirit. If you involve yourselves in sex now, not only will you be sinning against God and His perfect plan for your lives, but you will also be quenching the Spirit so you won't be able to discern if God would even want you to marry each other. Does that make sense?"

The look on Estevan's face told me he comprehended what I was saying. He took it to heart and then said, "I understand. I get it."

With that, Estevan seemed relieved to better understand the reasons for Steve's reservations about allowing them alone time.

Eventually, Estevan and Kayla grew up and were married. On the day they walked down the aisle as husband and wife, they were so grateful that the adults in their life helped them remain pure for marriage.

Having the courage to initiate difficult conversations is important. But if you have not developed a habit of talking to your son, where should you begin?

A great way to inspire your son to talk is to ask him something like, "If you could ask me any question right now, what would it be?" Be prepared for anything. You never know what your son might say! He may ask about something you are ready and willing to discuss, or he may ask, "Where do babies come from?"

One day when Brandon was in fifth grade, he surprised me and asked, "Mom, what's sex?" At the time Brandon came seeking answers to the age-old question, Steve was at work. I tried to say something that would hold him off until his father came home, but Brandon would not have it. I took a breath, whispered a prayer for wisdom, and sat down to reply to Brandon's questions about procreation.

At first, I went about explaining the act of intercourse like a junior high school biology teacher. I was quite pleased with myself as I finished the conversation. I was confident that Brandon now understood how babies were made. However, my usually quiet little guy was exceptionally talkative and inquisitive when it came to this topic. He asked why an unmarried woman we knew had become "pregnant by accident."

So then I had to explain how God created sex not only for procreation, but also as a pleasurable experience for husband and wife to enjoy. I shared with Brandon how the world exploits the sexual experience God had intended for married people, and how men sometimes have sex with women they do not love or do not want to marry simply because of the pleasure sex provides. I explained that any sexual relationship outside of the marriage bed is disobedience to God, and is sin.

I told Brandon, "Sometimes an unmarried woman will have sex with a man because she loves him and wants him to love her. When a woman gives herself to a man who is not committed to her, she often feels used and rejected." I continued, "Consider how one of your sisters would feel if a man ever used her in that way." Brandon agreed that a godly man would never do such a thing.

Our conversation went on for some time. At the end of it, Brandon and I bowed down in prayer, and I encouraged him to ask God to help him remain sexually pure for marriage, and to pray for the purity of the woman he would one day marry. When I thought Brandon was coming to the end of his prayer, he said, "Oh, and Lord, please protect my sisters from any boys ever using them for sex." (Even now those words bring a tear to my eye.)

Because Brandon heard about sex from me, I was able to help him see how women feel about sex and the effect immorality has upon them. And Brandon learned the importance of valuing a woman's purity as well. How precious that Brandon comprehended not only the need to obey the Lord with his sexuality, but also the need to never be the kind of man who uses women for his own sexual pleasure.

Since that day, Brandon and I have had many discussions about girls, dating, and sex. With an ethical, reverent attitude, Steve and I together have been privileged to help Brandon develop a biblical view of sexuality. Brandon says he has been thankful for my female perspective on the subject. If when Brandon was young I had danced around and avoided answering his questions about sex, I might have sent him the message, "Mom's not comfortable talking to you about sex, so don't ever bring it up again." If I had succumbed to my discomfort about discussing the subject with Brandon, I might have never had another opportunity to speak to him on this all-too-important topic.

Don't Be Naïve

If you and other godly adults in your son's life are reluctant to have transparent discussions with him about sex, he will end up going to other sources for information. The message he picks up from teachers, peers, music, and the media will likely teach him that sex before marriage is acceptable. Don't be naïve about how the world's philosophy regarding sex can influence your son. Your input is vital!

At every turn, the world has a casual attitude about sex. If all you do to help your son remain pure through his adolescent years is try to shelter him from exposure to sexual immorality, you will have taught him nothing. It is your job to influence your son's perceptions and understanding so that he can go out into the world prepared to stand against sexual seduction. Having open communication with your son when he asks questions or faces temptation will provide you with opportunities to teach him God's views about sex.

When your son shows interest in a girl, don't tell him, "You're too young to like a girl." Rather, talk with him about his feelings. Acknowledge the girl is lovely, and that she should be honored as God's creation. Rather than scold your son for admiring her beauty, help him learn to have God-honoring thoughts about the girl.

If you chastise your son for being attracted to the opposite sex, you will not discourage his attraction. What's more, you will likely not hear from him when he shows interest in a girl in the future, because he will not want to be made to feel guilty.

> **Don't be naïve about how the world's philosophy regarding sex can influence your son. Your input is vital!**

How much better it is for you to be involved in this normal part of his growing up, helping him to discern God's perspective about sex versus Satan's distortion of it.

One of the best ways to expose your son to a biblical view of sexual intimacy is to involve him in a church youth group in which he will learn the whole counsel of God from the Bible. Exposure to youth leaders who support a scriptural basis for sexual purity will help sow seeds of virtue in your son's mind. If the majority of your son's social activities are church-based, he is likely to make friends with other kids who are learning the same values, and whose parents hold to scriptural standards as well. You would be wise to establish relationships with parents who will join with you in providing supervised fellowship for your children.

What's more, do not be naïve about how strong a teenage boy's sexual drive can be. Allowing him to be alone with a girl in a secluded place is most definitely a recipe for indiscretion. In his immaturity, your son will likely believe he can contain his sexual passions. Teach him how even godly people can fall into sexual temptation by reading to him the Bible's account of David and Bathsheba (2 Samuel 11).

Satan is a roaring lion seeking to devour whomever he can (1 Peter 5:8). So train your son to defend himself against immorality by submitting to Scripture, resisting situations that might cause him to succumb to sexual temptation, and drawing near to God (James 4:7-8).

What's at Stake?

You and your son must understand just how serious sexual immorality is. It dishonors Christ and quenches the Spirit in his life. When your son is not being Spirit-led, he becomes vulnerable to Satan's deceptions and prone to succumbing to sin and evil.

Proverbs 11:18-19 promises, "He who sows righteousness will have a sure reward. As righteousness leads to life." For an example of how God honors righteous living, share with your son about Joseph. When Joseph, who was a slave in Egypt, was sexually seduced by the wife of his master, he literally ran away from her. Because of Joseph's faithful obedience and his pursuit of purity, the Lord eventually made him second in command over all of Egypt. Help your son make the connection that just as the Lord rewarded Joseph for living righteously, God will care for and lead your son if he obeys the Lord and resists sexual temptations.

As a mother, you have the wonderful opportunity to teach your son how to talk about the important issues of life. Do all you can to establish an environment conducive to good conversations by asking pertinent questions, being a good listener, and speaking God's wisdom to him in a kind and loving manner. The more you let God's Word dwell richly in you and you walk in obedience to the

Lord, the better prepared you will be to have meaningful discussions with your son. When you are equipped with wisdom from God's Word, the Spirit will enable you to listen to your son and to speak to him in ways that honor the Lord and draw your son to hear His truth.

With all the unbiblical influence our kids receive regarding romance, it is important that you train yourself how to teach your teens God's plan for romance. Let's look at six ways you can teach your teen.

Six Ways to Teach Teens about Real-Life Romance

In 18 years of youth ministry, my husband and I learned a lot about teens falling in love. In fact, I've enjoyed watching countless couples fall in love. I consider it a perk of being in ministry! I especially loved observing God's blessing on those who honored Christ in their romance. I can honestly attest to the value of exposing our children to real-life love stories that glorified Christ. Our children's idea of godly romance was strongly influenced by watching couples who loved God and obeyed His plan for their love lives.

In a generation where the culture has stolen real romance and where "anything goes" when it comes to sex, we must look for opportunities to talk to our teens and model for them love that brings glory to God. How can we expose them to romance that honors Christ? As a parent, you must realize that teaching your kids a biblical view of romance is so much more than just having "The Talk."

1. Acknowledge their longing to be in love.

It's tempting to tell your pimply-faced adolescent, "You're too young to have those feelings." But a wise parent will listen to them as they share their heart. If you shut them down, they'll still have those feelings; they just won't tell you about them. You'll also forfeit the opportunity to guide their thinking toward purity and biblical romance.

2. Talk plainly to them about sex.

This equips them for purity. How far is too far? Bottom line: It's all sex. Short of intercourse, everything that couples attempt to do outside of marriage is foreplay. There's no way around it. Your kids are naïve when they're messing around in the back seat of a car, telling themselves, *I'll know when to stop. I can handle this.* Help them understand they are engaged in foreplay, and their minds are preparing their bodies for intercourse. Eventually they will give in to sex before marriage.

Tell your kids that sex is amazing. Sidestepping the idea of how pleasurable sex can be will only serve to frustrate them. Rather, acknowledge how intercourse and all that leads up to the act is extremely enjoyable and sanctioned by God for married couples to enjoy. Equipping your teen to understand how God made their bodies to enjoy sex (within the safety of His plan) will keep them from one day being surprised by how much they long for physical intimacy with a person they come to have feelings for.

Your kids should know that it's possible to wait, even though culture says everyone is having sex. God's remnant is remaining pure until marriage, and He is blessing a whole new generation for their obedience. Exposing your kids to godly young adults who are waiting until marriage will speak more to them than your words.

But remind your kids that even if they fail, they can be pure again. God promises, "Though your sins are like scarlet, they shall be as white as snow" (Isaiah 1:18). If your child has been sexually active, hold out the hope of Jesus. Show the purity He offers to all who cry out to Him in repentance and turn from their sin.

3. Expose them to real romance.

Beginning with your own marriage, show your kids how romance in marriage is the norm rather than the exception. Expose your kids to couples in your church who are courting in a way that honors Christ. This helps them believe purity really is possible, contrary to what the world would have them think.

If you're a divorced or single parent, don't point out all the ways their other parent failed you in the relationship. Instead, expose your kids to marriages that have grown more deeply in love over the years. The best place to find these godly examples of happy marriages is when you become a part of a church family. This requires regularly attending church—not just popping in on Sundays from time to time.

4. Celebrate true love.

Telling your kids stories of how God sovereignly brought two people together to fall in love in a Christ-honoring way gives them hope that God is also interested in their happily-ever-after. When they believe that letting God write their love story will guide them to romance with no regrets, they'll be more likely to trust Him and wait on His timing when looking for a spouse. (For Christ-honoring true love stories for your teens read my book, *Real-Life Romance*.)

5. Help them realize their longing to feel loved is normal.

God created each of us with a longing to find our worth in who loves us. The problem lies in looking to find our worth in how well a significant other treats us. The ache we have to feel treasured can only be satisfied when we realize that God loves us so much that He sent His Son to purchase us for Himself. The intimacy with the Creator was stolen away when mankind sinned in the garden. From then on, we all search for love in the wrong places. God is the only answer to the longing of our hearts.

6. Tell him to find a woman who loves God more than she loves him.

She'll be a wife who will love with God's love! The Bible instructs believers not to marry unbelievers. Why? One very important reason is because the only people who have the capacity to love others with Christ's selfless love are those whose hearts have been transformed by the Holy Spirit.

We regularly told our own children as well as our youth ministry kids, "Marry someone who loves Jesus more than they love you, and you're on the right track to a marriage that will last a lifetime."

Telling our kids how not to feel will do nothing to guide their hearts. But exposing them to real, Christ-honoring romance will kindle a spark of hope that God really is sovereign over romance and love.

Mom, your example in the area of sexual purity is vital. I cannot stress enough the damage a mother's sexual immorality can have upon her son. If you have sex outside of marriage, not only will your sin likely cause your son to stumble in the area of his own purity, but your sin will quench the Spirit in your life, and your parenting will be done in the flesh—not by the power of the Holy Spirit working through you. No matter what today's culture says, don't be deceived. You will reap what you sow if you sow seeds of immorality (Galatians 6:7-9).

Sex Is Spiritual

If you've ever studied the concept of covenant in Scripture, you will see how the practice of cutting a covenant involved two individuals passing between two pieces of flesh as a sign of their covenant. Think of God cutting the covenant with Abram in Genesis 15. In the same way, intercourse (the passing between the flesh) is God's intended sign of the marriage covenant that knits two souls together as one in the eyes of God (Malachi 2:13-14).

In a world that speaks to the contrary, we must teach this generation that sex is not just sex. It's God's beautiful way of knitting two hearts together to become one. For many years my husband, Steve, and I taught on sexual purity at youth events. In my session with the girls, I'd glue together two construction paper hearts—one pink and one blue. Then I'd hold up the heart, and while the glue dried, I'd explain God's beautiful plan for sexual intimacy.

I'd say, "Imagine you are the pink heart. And you gave yourself to a young man represented by the blue heart. But then when you broke up"—I'd begin to tear apart the two hearts—"pieces of his blue heart have been left on your pink, and your pink on his blue. Get the point?" I'd continue, "Each time a person joins themselves sexually with someone outside of marriage, pieces of their heart are stripped away. Only God can make that heart whole again. By the time a person is ready to marry, their hearts are either in one piece because they've honored Christ, or they have only a fragmented heart to offer their spouse."

This simple illustration had a powerful impact on my audience. And it provided a wonderful opportunity to share with them how Jesus came to wash all our sins as far as the east is from the west, making us whiter than snow if one would repent and surrender to Christ as their Lord and Savior. I've used this same illustration when talking with our children about sex because it seems to help teens visualize what the Bible teaches in Mark 10:8, where Jesus said, "And the two shall become one flesh; so then they are no longer two, but one flesh."

This is an important concept to instill in your children. Because the world's cavalier attitude toward casual sexual encounters can tempt your child toward immorality, you would do well to help them understand sex is an act of marriage that solidifies the couple's covenant.[1]

Helping your child honor the Lord with their sexuality is by far one of the most intimidating tasks as a parent. However, consider the privilege God is granting you to help your son understand how God created sex to be enjoyed without shame in the bonds of marriage. And to what God has called you, He promises to help you. So ask God to grant you His courage and wisdom to have with your son the difficult conversations about sexuality.

In my experience, being willing to answer our children's questions while they were young paid off abundantly when later in life my children were comfortable to openly discuss with me the sexual temptations they were facing. Know this: Your son's openness to advice, prayer, and accountability shouldn't begin on the day he is in over his head. Rather, your healthy communication—based upon a foundation of candid, age-appropriate, biblical conversations about sex and purity—will lay the groundwork for him to invite your advice.

THINKING IT THROUGH

Whatever age your son is now, consider how you might help him establish a biblical worldview of romance and dating. What conversations might you have with him when he inadvertently observes inappropriate romance on television or social media?

LIVING IT OUT

The Bible says if anyone lacks wisdom, ask God for it, and He will give it freely (James 1:5). Write out a prayer of petition. Ask God to give you wisdom and discernment to train your son to guard his heart and pursue only Christ-honoring purity.

Watch this chapter's video teaching at
www.rhondastoppe.com/books/moms-raising-sons-to-be-men.

CHAPTER 15

EVEN IF YOU'RE ALONE

Hope and Help for Single Moms

My friend Linda was raised in a loving Christian home. Her parents were both very involved in their church. She had always gone to Sunday school, vacation Bible school, youth group, and church camps. Pretty much whatever the church had to offer, she was in attendance. She had received Christ as a young girl and knew many memory verses and the names of all the books of the Bible by heart. Everything seemed to be just as it should be in Linda's life.

As a young adult, Linda began to socialize with people other than her church friends. And of course there was that guy—there's always a guy. He was charming, funny, and cute. How could there be anything wrong with spending time with him? He was not a believer, but Linda was determined he would become one. She invited him to church activities, and he came. Who says missionary dating doesn't work? Linda was crazy about Stan, and he was just as crazy about her.

Gradually Stan began to pull Linda away from her Christian

friends. The Lord was convicting Linda about her choices, but she so wanted to please Stan that she filled her quiet times with distractions and tuned out the still, small voice of the Lord.

It wasn't too long into their dating relationship that Linda became pregnant. Stan asked Linda to marry him. After visiting with Linda's pastor, Stan walked the aisle in church, prayed a prayer, and poof, called himself a Christian. Now they could get married, and everything would be all right…or so Linda wanted to believe.

Within months, Linda and Stan had a bouncing baby boy. A year-and-a-half later, they had another beautiful son. Although things were tight financially, everything seemed fine. Until Stan began to disappear for days at a time, and their finances dwindled for no apparent reason.

One day Linda was shocked to discover that Stan had developed an overwhelming addiction to cocaine. He appeared to be a nice, clean-cut young man who loved his family and held a good job, but frequently he would binge, living a completely different life than the one he had at home with his loving wife and two precious sons.

Linda truly loved her husband, and her heart broke as she watched him destroy himself. She pleaded with Stan to get help, but to no avail. For some time he had refused to attend church with Linda and the boys. Linda's pastor helped her come to the difficult decision to move herself and her sons out of the unhealthy environment at home.

Linda could not believe her life had turned out this way. She came from a godly family. She had loved the Lord and wanted nothing more than to be the wife of a godly man and raise children who loved the Lord. Why had she not seen the warning signs in Stan? How did things get so out of control? And where would she turn from here?

She turned to her God.

Sadly, Linda's husband eventually took his own life. She had long since repented of her own rebellion against the Lord and had determined to live for Him, making it her main priority to raise her sons to know and love the Lord. Linda would be the first to tell you that God can take our messes and use them for His glory. She often warns women of the painful consequences of choosing to disobey God's instruction to remain sexually pure.

How is it possible in this age to follow God's laws for sexual purity? In her book *Idols of the Heart*, Elyse Fitzpatrick states: "The problem is not that we need to develop more willpower. The problem is that we need new thoughts, new inclinations, and new desires. We don't need to learn how to pull ourselves up by our bootstraps or 'gut it out.' We need to seek to replace our sinful passions with holy ones. When God grants these new holy passions to us, we'll find that our will, which seemed so weak before, will joyfully comply."[1]

I have been friends with Linda for over 30 years. She is one of the best mothers I have ever known (and now she is an incredible grandmother too!). I have learned much from this wise and godly woman. Both of her sons, now adults, love and serve the Lord.

Although as a young woman Linda chose to rebel against the Lord, she returned to obediently follow His leading. Her sons were not destined to be ungodly, rebellious men who used drugs simply because their father had done so. In cultivating her love for God, by example, she was able to teach her sons to love Him as well. God truly is faithful to make all things work together for good.

Single Mom, Take Heart

If you are divorced but your son's father is still involved in his life, be careful to speak with respect about his dad. I know one divorced mother whose son never knew his successful father had a drug addiction. She was careful to allow her son supervised interaction with his dad, and wisely determined not to tear down her son's father. As the years passed, her son matured into a man who learned of his father's drug issues. Filtered through the strong foundation of Scripture laid by his mother, the young man was able to assess his father's choices, recognize how wrong they were, and forgive his father.

It is natural for your son to have an admiration for his dad. When you point out your ex-husband's failures, your son may respond with feelings of resentment toward you for tearing down his father. Do not put your son in a place where he feels he must constantly choose which parent he will align himself with. When your son reaches adolescence, you just may lose.

If your son has experienced deep wounds or negligence at the hands of his father, teach your son to forgive his father. (You may need to repent of your own resentment as well.) Help your son focus on how as a Christian he is part of the family of God through his relationship with Christ, rather than on how his father's absence has wounded him. Teach him that rather than being consumed by his scars, he can find freedom at the cross.

Raising up a son is made more difficult when you are a single mom—making it even more important that you glorify God as a mother and call your son to honor God as he obeys you. Psalm 68:5 says the Lord is "a father of the fatherless." As you walk closely with God, He will be faithful to His Word about being Father of the fatherless and help you raise your son.

I have a friend who was a single mother of two sons. I have known Sherry since her boys were very young. Over the years Sherry has diligently worked on two major relationships: intimacy with God and intimacy with her sons. She took seriously God's promise to be Father to her fatherless sons, and knew He would be the One to help her gain their obedient respect. She taught her sons that when they were obeying their mom, they were obeying God—which is the greatest motivation we can give our children for being obedient. Sherry also spent a great deal of time building a thriving, loving relationship with her boys.

The results of Sherry's diligence became evident when her sons became adolescents. Along with trusting the Lord to help her earn the love and respect of her boys, Sherry wisely looked to her church for godly men who could serve as mentors for her sons. She wanted the boys to have heroes they could look up to. How better to find God-fearing men than to ask the Lord to direct her sons to men in the church? Now in their thirties, Sherry's sons can look back and name several Christian men who taught them to be men who honored the Lord—and their mother.

When looking for men who could mentor your son, look for men who have a genuine passion for Christ. Don't find men who simply follow religious rules. Rather, try to find men who are faithful and consistent in exhibiting Christlike character. The young men of this generation ache for heroes who are genuine, passionate, and noble. Determine to expose your son to men who sincerely love the Lord and passionately glorify Him.

You're in Good Company

Acts 16:1 tells us Timothy's mother, Eunice, had been married to a Greek man. We are not told whether Timothy's father had been a Christian. The original Greek text of Acts 16:1 suggests Timothy's Gentile father may have been dead by the time Eunice met the apostle Paul. Eunice may have been a widow, raising her son with the help of her mother. And God provided Paul as young Timothy's father-in-the-faith. The apostle shaped the life of Eunice's son in a way she never could.

Can you imagine the privilege of having the apostle Paul mentor your son? Not only did Paul disciple young Timothy, but he considered him a true son. To encourage Timothy, Paul wrote two letters to the young man who won the honor of being Paul's most cherished protégé.

When Paul knew the time of his death was near, he expressed his great desire to see Timothy once more before he died. I don't know about you, but just contemplating their plight brings tears to my eyes. How Timothy's heart must have ached when he opened the precious letter from his godly mentor! How the tears must have streamed down Timothy's face as he read Paul's statement, "Greatly desiring to see you, being mindful of your tears" (2 Timothy 1:4).

With a sense of urgency, Paul penned a letter passing the mantle of his ministry to Timothy. All through the letter of 2 Timothy, Paul delivered exhortations to Timothy to preach the gospel diligently, and to guard the sound doctrine he had received from the apostle. But before he laid out those instructions, Paul took time to celebrate the heritage of Timothy's faith that came from two wonderful women: "[I am] filled with joy, when I call to remembrance the genuine faith that is in you, which dwelt first in your grandmother Lois and your mother Eunice, and I am persuaded is in you also" (2 Timothy 1:4-5).

When it came time for Paul to hand the baton of ministry to the next generation, he gave it to his beloved Timothy. Wouldn't you love for the Lord to send a godly "father in the faith" to prepare your son to minister to his generation? Have you asked the Lord? Will you ask Him now?

Whether you are married or a single mom, the more you expose your son to men who glorify the Lord, the more opportunities your son will have to develop his own identity through their godly influence.

You Are Not Alone

Even though you may feel like you're the only one raising kids without a spouse, statistics reveal you are not alone. But far beyond the comfort of knowing there are many other single moms out there who have the same struggles as you, you should be happy to know you are not alone because God says you are not!

Psalm 68:5 says the Lord is a father of the fatherless. Just meditate on that for a minute. Your partner in parenting is *God Himself*! Years ago I shared this promise with a young man whose father had died of a drug overdose. When this young man heard that God promised to be Father to him because he was fatherless, he was filled with relief, courage, and hope for the future.

So Mom—what's your part? You likely didn't plan on being a single mom, right? Most single moms find themselves ill-prepared for the situation in which they find themselves. But be encouraged; God has walked with single moms down through the ages, and He will walk with you too—if you determine to draw near to Him. In Isaiah 41:10, God says:

> Fear not, for I am with you;
> Be not dismayed, for I am your God;
> I will strengthen you,
> Yes, I will help you,
> I will uphold you with My righteous right hand.

How exciting is that? God Himself promises to help you! So memorize Isaiah 41:10. And when those anxious times arise—and they will—recite aloud this verse. Pray these words to the Lord and remind Him of His promise to help you. And then, watch and see how He will work mightily on your behalf.

THINKING IT THROUGH

What did you learn about Timothy's mother, Eunice (2 Timothy 1:5)?

How will your practice of sexual purity empower your son to guard his own virginity?

Consider how your discipline in this area will visit blessing upon you and your children for generations to come.

LIVING IT OUT

If you're a single mom, don't fret. History records countless hardworking, godly men who were raised by a single mother without a father's affirmation. What steps will you take to expose your son to godly mentors?

Watch this chapter's video teaching at
www.rhondastoppe.com/books/moms-raising-sons-to-be-men.

CHAPTER 16

EVEN IF YOU'RE SCARED

Facing the Culture War with
Wisdom and Strength

There is a push in the Christian community to care so much about social justice that we are in danger of missing our true calling. We want to raise kids who care about sharing the gospel, about living as light. When they are walking in a relationship with Christ, His Holy Spirit in them will cause our children to move toward both loving and helping people. It is Christ in us, the hope of glory, who moves us toward caring for others.

Moms, there is a movement, even in our pulpits, to focus on culture and miss the main purpose to which God is calling us. Many mainstream pastors are moving away from preaching expository sermons from biblical passages toward sociology conversations with their congregations. Conversations, rather than biblical preaching, have no power to transform lives or have lasting influence upon a culture for a godly cause. You must be discerning about the type of teaching that you and your children are getting in church and from their youth pastors.

It is vital for your son's development toward godly manhood that he is being transformed by truth rather than manipulated by influential conversations—because the Word of God is sharp and powerful and can ignite your son toward God's kingdom purpose for his life.

What Is the Culture War?

It's fair to say that every generation has wrestled with conflicts of ideals, beliefs, and philosophies. In Ecclesiastes 1:9, King Solomon was correct when he wisely stated, "There is nothing new under the sun." About a thousand years after Solomon penned the book of Ecclesiastes, the apostle Paul faced horrendous injustices in *his* culture. While facing his own culture war, Paul wisely determined to stay true to his cause by choosing not to preach against the injustices, but rather to offer hope in his generation by proclaiming boldly the gospel of Jesus Christ. While Christians were being slaughtered, slavery, prostitution, and sex trafficking were rampant. And amid his own unjust sufferings, Paul proclaimed, "We preach Christ crucified" (1 Corinthians 1:23).

Let the main thing be the main thing. And the main thing is training your son to love God with all his being so that Jesus's love will spill out of his actions.

This is a great reminder, Momma: *Let the main thing be the main thing.* And the main thing is training your son to love God with all his being so that Jesus's love will spill out of his actions. This wholehearted devotion to the Lord is God's path to your son's life of purpose, passion, and godly influence in his culture. And this is true for you too.

In our society, social injustices are occurring at an alarming rate. And political unrest is uprooting much of what we hold dear. But obsession over these things can hijack your godly passions, which will derail your motivation to spread the only message that can offer reconciliation and hope—the gospel.

In Mark 12:28-34, Jesus explained how wholehearted devotion to God is the key to loving others well. A person is only able to love their neighbor selflessly if they have a deep, abiding love for God. So training your son how to grow his love for God is essential. This is how the Lord transforms a society with Christ's love—one person at a time.

The cause is Christ. Make Him known to a generation desperate to believe that there is a God who created them, loves them, and has a purpose for their lives. There is only one just God who can make right the injustices in our world—and that begins with genuine love and obedience to Christ. Let it begin with you.

A Distorted View of Freedom

Your son may develop a distorted view of freedom if you allow him to govern himself. You should help him mature into a man who will eventually be independent from *your* authority, but *never* independent from God's authority. As you train your son to honor your God-given position of leadership, you will help mold him into a man who respects the Lord's authority, as well as the authorities God has placed over him in our culture.

I mentioned earlier in this book how sons approaching manhood long to feel respected. So don't be surprised if your son triggers in anger or pushes you away when he feels like you are not giving him enough freedom. His idea of freedom, influenced by the culture, will be distorted and self-serving. It's your job to help him realize how to live in true freedom by honoring the Lord's commands and submitting to the authorities He places over your son.

Video Games and Pseudo-Success

The culture's influence will train your son to either resist work or run hard after success at the expense of relationships and godly integrity. Sadly, most young men today fall in one of two opposite extremes. There are those who idolize their work, finding their

identity in their accomplishments. They are willing to do whatever it takes to get ahead by putting self before others. Then there
are those who are lazy and hate to work. They rely on their parents for financial help while they pursue entertainment or personal
pleasures.

King Solomon had this to say about work: "He who tills his land
will be satisfied with bread, but he who follows frivolity is devoid
of understanding" (Proverbs 12:11). Solomon meant anyone who
spends time on worthless pursuits and fantasies is ignorant. Does
that remind you of anything? It makes me think of video games. I
know many young adult men who are addicted to video games.
Finding a sense of accomplishment when they reach the next level,
their God-instilled propensity to work and conquer are somehow
fed in a sort of pseudo-satisfaction.

Now please do not take that to mean you should go throw out
all your son's video games. That is *not* my point. The problem isn't
necessarily the video games themselves, but the extended use of
them. Anything done to an extreme can be addictive, so you want
to use wisdom and discernment with regard to the amount of time
your son plays video games and the types of games he is allowed
to have. Ask the Holy Spirit to help you discern what is and is not
acceptable.

You can use your son's access to video games as a tool to teach
him how to *monitor himself.* It is wise to allow certain freedoms so
your son can learn to be self-disciplined and self-motivated concerning how he spends his time. Rather than removing all possible
time-wasting temptations, use wholesome entertainment options as
a way to train your son to regulate his use of time. Even thoroughly
wholesome entertainment requires the use of discernment. Training your son to determine what is right and best will prepare him to
govern himself well when he is grown.

When you talk to your son about video games, use your discussion to teach him how and why he should be in charge of his free

time. Let him know you're not opposed to him playing video games. Rather, it's his management of time and the kinds of games he plays that you're concerned about.

How might your son respond if you assured him you understand how much he enjoys playing video games? What if you took the time to explain that gaming in itself is not wrong? But then carefully point out that feasting for hours on games and exposing oneself to excessive violence are inappropriate. Taking his thought process further, give your son an opportunity to see how Satan could use video games, or other amusements, to squelch his incentive to accomplish good with his life.

As you instruct your son, remind him God has given you the position of authority over him. And because you want to help him grow mature and wise, you want him to see how some activities may hurt him later in life. It is your job as a parent to help him see those things as well so he can learn how to guard himself.

Beware of being *too* extreme. The all-or-nothing approach may seem easier in the moment, but it will not build your son's ability to exercise discernment and keep watch over how he spends his time. Remember, your son's desire is to grow toward independence as a man, so appeal to the man he will be rather than proclaim your authority to dictate his choices. Ultimately you and his father have the right to enforce regulations on the amount of time your son spends with video games and other pursuits. But consider teaching your son to think through the negative impact of time wasted on unproductive or worthless activities, and involve him in that thought process. After you've done that, maybe together you could come up with a reasonable amount of time for him to spend on video games. (And Momma, if you have a true conviction against letting your children play video games, you would be wise to obey the Lord's leading for your family.)

Your goal is to make your son see that you are on his side, and that your desire is to help him become a man who does not squander his time and his talents on temporal pleasures. When you train your son to self-discipline himself in this way, it will help him in *every* area of his life—not just in matters of personal entertainment.

Who Am I? How Do I Fit In?

Kids ache to belong. I remember when our eldest son, Tony, became our son. His childhood had been overshadowed by rejection and pain. Finding ways to teach Tony his worth in Christ was key to his mental well-being. Along with his surrender to Christ as his Savior, Tony grew secure as he came to believe that we were his family—for better or worse. He belonged to us, and nothing would cause us to reject him.

Tony's story is not uncommon among teens. Sadly, for many teens, their longing to fit with their peers is cause for depression, anxiety, and fear of rejection. Social media has hijacked real relationship building for a virtual interaction that comes up empty. If they're posting all their happy photos online while secretly aching inside, their loneliness will be compounded. And when teens work hard to put forth a particular social media persona, they may struggle with imposter syndrome, causing some to be afraid to let anyone get too close—to unveil their true identity. If parents are busy with work or other pressing matters, adolescents tend to feel even more isolated and alone, so they bury themselves in video games or virtual relationships. This loneliness can lead to depression and destructive behavior.

About 25 years ago, when Steve was a youth pastor in a very wealthy community, there was a slew of teen suicides. These children appeared to be living their best lives with the good things in life at their fingertips. Sadly, when those possessions could not fill the void, they turned to substances and other experiences that left them empty. When one committed suicide, it triggered other suicides among their peers.

One mother of a boy who took his own life said, "Please tell parents about this. Please warn them to pay attention to the signs. And tell them get help before it's too late."

As I considered this topic, I happened upon a radio interview between our dear friends at Dr. James Dobson's Family Institute. I learned so much from that episode. And since I am not a licensed counselor, I thought, with their permission, I'd let the experts help us out by sharing with you excerpts from the show's transcript: "Preventing Teen Suicide: Kids in Crisis with Dr. Tim Clinton and Dr. James Dobson."[1]

Clinton: People have often said to me, "Why do these kids go out and party like they do? Why are they getting so messed up with drugs and alcohol and stuff?" And some of it is experimentation...But for many of them, Dr. Dobson, you're right; it's peer pressure. But how about just filling the emptiness in the soul? If you're made for relationship and your relationships are broken, they're not working, you're going to reach for something else to anesthetize or to fill the hole in your soul...Developmentally, they're wrestling with questions like, "Who am I? How do I fit in?" When you...don't have anybody to talk to, and then it starts getting dark for you, and then you start thinking about these internet experiences or games, or you start watching this show [about teen suicide], you start getting lost in your own mind.

Dobson: You know how it gets manifested—that message of hope that God's there? It comes through Mom, Dad, a youth pastor, a grandpa, a coach...Somebody owning their influence in the life of a child, in the life of a teen. Somebody who's willing to...say, "You know what? This is what I love about you. What I like about you, is everything.

I'm here for you. Listen to me, son…There's not one thing you can't come to me and talk about…" And we get that kind of emotional closeness and connection by what? By being present, by being attuned to our son or daughter. If you are distracted or if you are working long hours, and are worn-out when you get home, if you are too involved in your own world to see what's happening in your sons and daughters, if you ignore them, if they are not part of your inner being, if you don't take the time to love them, I will promise you that the culture will take your kids to hell, one way or another. You can't afford to do that. You will miss the most important thing in life if you invest it all in a career opportunity. I know it is tempting when you've gone to college and you've got this education and you're offered a job and it makes you work or travel too much, or you're gone too much, that you don't notice, right around your feet, some kid is crying for you and reaching for you, but you don't have time for them. This kind of thing is more likely to happen. You've got to convey worth, value, and meaning to them. You've got to let them know that they matter to you. And I don't care what you accomplish in life, if you don't get that done, you have failed.

Clinton: I know some are probably asking, "What do you do?" First of all, connect. And don't get overwhelmed or lost in it. Be deliberate, be intentional. One of the great myths here is to think that if I talk about suicide, then I'm going to place those seeds into his or her heart. That is not true. It's the opposite. Go right into it, and if you have an indication that they are contemplating suicide…don't leave them alone, continue to talk with them. And then, you're right, get them help, or the hopelessness will take them out. You get on the phone with 911, you get them to an emergency room, you get them to a professional counselor immediately. Especially if you're seeing this high-risk behavior taking place, because this is real. And the good news is, if you do that, you can save a heart. You can save a life. Usually it isn't that they hate life. It's just that they hate life the way it is.

Dobson: I had a dad who believed in me and told me he did.

Clinton: Own your influence! That word goes out to every coach, it goes out to every dad, to every pastor, to everybody who has influence in the life of a teen. So if we're talking about teen suicide, own your influence in their life. Stop turning them away. Recognize that God's placed them there for a reason. And if you do, you may avert a teen suicide. It could be because *you* showed up and *you* spoke hope, truth, love into their life.

Dobson: I had a Sunday school teacher, a man that we all loved. Every student in his class absolutely loved him. He had great influence in our life. Somebody like that can save a boy or girl in trouble.

Clinton: That's soul-care ministry; showing up, letting God work through you to bring His comfort and hope to them.

Take a Breath

I know teen suicide is a burdensome topic most parents don't want to think about. But anyone who has worked with youth will tell you how prevalent suicide has become among teens, so don't be naïve about your own child's vulnerability, or that of their friends. The National Institute of Mental Health website states that suicide is the second leading cause of death among individuals between the ages of 10 and 34.[2] This information is heartbreaking. But if you are a Christ follower, you can be an ambassador of hope to a hopeless child by showing up, listening, talking, and letting God work through you to bring His comfort and hope to your son, to his friends, or whomever God sends your way.

You must have the courage to talk to your son about the deceptive mindset in our culture that suicide is a way of escape. Having the hard conversations with a child who's feeling alone will help him to believe, *Someone is listening. Someone cares. Someone is going to show up and walk me through this dark valley toward hope, purpose, and life.*

Talking about suicide unmasks Satan's lies and can equip your son to recognize if the enemy attempts to seduce him or his friends toward self-destruction. You would be wise to have your son involved in a church youth group where the youth leaders listen, teach biblically, and build relationships with them. This interaction can play a vital role in helping your son learn how much God loves him. And this fellowship can help your son know that he is not alone when he faces dark times.

Please don't allow this conversation about suicide to paralyze you with fear. Remember, "He who is in you is greater than he who is in the world" (1 John 4:4). Jesus said, "Behold, I send you out as sheep in the midst of wolves. Therefore be as wise as serpents and harmless as doves" (Matthew 10:16). So if your son goes through a dark season, ask God to grant you His courage, wisdom, and gentleness to pursue him. And if your son pushes you away, press in even more to show him your unconditional love. Finally, seek out the help of certified biblical counselors, youth pastors, and godly mentors. You can obtain free counseling at www.focusonthefamily.com/get-help.

Secularism has an enormous influence on our culture and parenting. But this is the world in which you are raising your son to be a man, so this is where you must be prepared. It is vital that you discipline yourself to learn truth from the Bible and godly teachers so you won't be swayed by manipulative narratives.

When you love God with your whole heart, your son will likely be drawn toward you and your genuine faith. And with Christ loving your son through you, you can show him in practical ways how deeply he is valued and adored by you, and more importantly, by God Himself.

This Is Your Time

In 1950, when missionary Jim Elliot decided to leave the safety of America to take the gospel to the native peoples of the Ecuadoran jungle, his parents were fearful for his safety. Confident that his decision was directed by the Lord, Jim wrote this in a letter to his parents: "Remember how the psalmist described children? He said that they were a heritage from the Lord, and that every man should be happy who had his quiver full of them. And what is a quiver full of but arrows? And what are arrows for but to shoot? So with the strong arms of prayer, draw the bowstring back and let the arrows fly—all of them, straight at the enemy's hosts."[3]

Are you doing what it takes to prepare the arrows in your quiver? As you apply the biblical principles you have learned in this book, you can help prepare your son for God's purposes. When it's time to pull back the bowstring and release your son, imagine tearfully watching him leave your bow. Holding your breath, you observe and pray as the Holy Spirit, like a mighty rushing wind, sovereignly guides him to the bull's-eye so that he might light on fire the generation in which the Lord ordained that he would live. I can think of no greater way to send my son out into the world—can you?

The influence of mothers has shaped nations, trained leaders, nurtured artists, and encouraged ordinary men to accomplish extraordinary feats. This is your time in history, Mom. This generation needs mothers who will selflessly embrace this blessed calling of motherhood and raise sons who are courageous and righteous.

A Word as We Part

My heart is so filled with hope for this generation, which will be influenced by your courage to raise your son to be a man. Motherhood matters. *You* matter! I pray this book has helped you become a courageous mother through whom God will do exceedingly and abundantly more than you can ask or imagine, as you raise your son in the nurture and admonition of the Lord. Soli Deo gloria!

THINKING IT THROUGH

Learning from godly mentors and growing mature in your walk with Christ is vital to your success as a mother. And we need you, Mom. This generation is desperate for moms who take seriously their calling to influence our culture through courageous righteous motherhood. To this, God has called you. And for this, He will empower you if you draw near to Christ, laying aside anything that would beset you so you can run the race that He has set before you. For His kingdom and His glory.

One final note: I implore you not to just put this book on the shelf. I pray that this will be a resource you look back over and ponder to help you guide your son toward godly manhood. And I'm praying you share this book with your friends. It's an ideal book and video series for a small group study, so please consider inviting other moms to join you. Also, please take time to submit a book review and to share a quote from the book in your social media; these are great ways to help me help mothers. Finally, please join my private Facebook group: *Moms Raising Sons to Be Men Book Club*. There you'll have access to me personally during my annual small group study.

LIVING IT OUT

Through these pages you have learned from mothers in the Bible, you've been inspired by moms whose influence changed history, and you've learned from experts how to guide your son toward a life without regrets. It has been a lot to take in, I know. But I am confident you have the fortitude to apply these biblical principles to raising your son toward manhood.

As intimidating as motherhood can be, remember that with God's help, you are not alone. Motherhood is one of the most valuable investments you'll ever make into your children, grandchildren, and future generations. I leave you with this path for success that God gave to Joshua when it was his turn to lead the children of Israel:

> Be strong and very courageous, that you may observe to do according to all the law which Moses My servant commanded you; do not turn from it to the right hand or to the left, that you may prosper wherever you go. This Book of the Law shall not depart from your mouth, but you shall meditate in it day and night, that you may observe to do according to all that is written in it. For then you will make your way prosperous, and then you will have good success. Have I not commanded you? Be strong and of good courage; do not be afraid, nor be dismayed, for the LORD your God is with you wherever you go (Joshua 1:7-9).

Watch this chapter's video teaching at
www.rhondastoppe.com/books/moms-raising-sons-to-be-men.

HOW TO HAVE A RELATIONSHIP WITH JESUS

"What on earth could she possibly mean by a *relationship* with Jesus?" you ask. I am so glad you want to know!

Did you know that God created people so He could have a relationship with them? When the Lord created Adam and Eve and put them in the garden of Eden, He did not leave them there with a list of religious rituals to perform while He observed from afar. No, Genesis 3:8 says that God walked with Adam and Eve "in the garden in the cool of the day." He spent time with them!

You have likely heard some form of the story of how God put a tree in the garden and commanded Adam and Eve not to eat of its fruit, or they would surely die (Genesis 2:17). Genesis 3 records how one day Satan came and tempted Eve to partake of the forbidden fruit. Eve was deceived and seduced by Satan's lies and ate the fruit—and of course Adam followed suit. In the moment they disobeyed God's command, not only did their bodies begin to die physically, but what's worse is that they died spiritually. Can you imagine how empty they must have felt when that happened?

You see, once Adam and Eve sinned, they rejected God's rule and yielded themselves to Satan. And without someone to rescue them, they were without hope of ever being in right standing with God again. Because of their rebellion against God, they could no longer fellowship with Him, for God cannot allow sin in His presence. And unless God provided a way that Adam and Eve—and by extension, all of mankind—could have that relationship restored, they would forever be without hope. Every one of us was destined to spend eternity in hell, separated from God's presence.

However, because of God's great love for His creation, He had planned a way to rescue us and bring us back to Himself. (That's why we use the word *salvation*!)

Have you ever wondered, *Why did God put that tree in the garden anyway? I mean, if it hadn't been there, Adam and Eve would never have been tempted.* Did Adam and Eve's sin catch God by surprise, so that the Trinity (God the Father, God the Son, and God the Holy Spirit) entered into a holy huddle to figure out Plan B for mankind's redemption? (*Redemption* is a big word that basically means "buy back"—see Revelation 5:9.) No—God knew Adam and Eve would fall. Revelation 13:8 says Jesus was "slain from the foundation of the world." That means even before God created the world or people, He knew all of us would need a Savior. And because of His great love for us, and His desire to have a people who would *choose* to love and serve Him, He put the tree in the garden to give Adam and Eve a choice. When they sinned (and He knew they would), God told them He would offer up His Son to pay the price for their disobedience (Romans 5:12-21).

Imagine—God loved us so much that He sacrificed His only Son, that whoever believes in Him will not die but will live forever (John 3:16)! God says the very act of offering His greatest treasure, Jesus, was His way of showing you and me just how very much He loves us. "God demonstrates His own love toward us, in that while we were still sinners, Christ died for us" (Romans 5:8).

So what does it mean to believe in Him like John 3:16 says? Is it a mere mental assent to the truth that Jesus is fully God, and being fully God He took on the form of a man when He was born through a virgin? And that Jesus lived a sinless life, willingly gave Himself up to die a cruel death on a cross, and then victoriously rose from the dead—so that His blood could wash away our sins and He could give us eternal life? While all those statements are true, if you simply *agree* with the facts about Jesus, that does not mean you have a *relationship* with Him. In fact, James 2:19 says even the demons believe, and they tremble in fear because they *know* who Jesus is, and what He accomplished when He died for our sins.

Having a relationship with Jesus is entering into a personal covenant (that's a big word that means "vow" or "promise") with Jesus. He wants us to make a lifelong commitment to Him—but how?

First, God wants you to repent of your sins. (*Repent* means to agree with God that you are a sinner in need of a Savior, and that you will turn away from your sins.) The Bible says, "All have sinned and fall short of the glory of God" (Romans 3:23). Only the blood of Jesus can wash away your sins (Hebrews 9:14).

I know it's easy to take offense when someone says, "You're a sinner," but let's be honest: You and I both know that even though we try to do what's right, our natural instinct is to disobey God's laws. You see, God gave us those laws *not* so we could try to become sinless by doing all that they command, but to show us that we will *never* be able to measure up to the sinless life God requires of us to have a relationship with Him and enter into heaven when we die (Galatians 2:16; 3:24).

So where does that leave us? If Galatians 2:16 says that no one is justified by the works of the law, then how can we possibly be restored to God and go to heaven? If God isn't making sure our good deeds outweigh our bad deeds by the time we die (a completely bogus concept not taught in Scripture), and if, as Romans 6:23 says, "The wages of sin is death," how can we be rescued from judgment?

I'm glad you asked! For the Bible also says, "The gift of God is eternal life in Christ Jesus our Lord" and that we are justified (made right) "by faith in Jesus Christ" (Romans 6:23; Galatians 2:16). The Bible teaches that Jesus is not simply one of many ways to salvation; He is the *only* way. In John 14:6, Jesus said, "I am the way, the truth, and the life. No one comes to the Father except through Me." Those are Jesus's words, not mine. The *only* way to an intimate relationship with God is through Jesus. It is only when you receive His free gift of salvation that Jesus's blood washes away all of your sins. God Himself says, "Though your sins are like scarlet, they shall be as white as snow" (Isaiah 1:18). Think of it—God promises to wipe the slate completely clean! No matter how many bad decisions you have made up to this point, no matter how shameful your past, Jesus is offering you freedom from all of it! Freedom from shame and the bondage of sin.

Once Jesus washes away your sins, He promises *never* to throw them in your face again. The Bible says God removes our sins from us "as far as the east is from the west" (Psalm 103:12). (You do realize that east and west never meet, right? That means that in Christ, our sins are taken away *forever*!)

But you don't get to just say some magic words, "I believe," and then go back to life as usual. Jesus says He wants you to surrender all that you are to Him. "If you confess with your mouth the Lord Jesus and believe in your heart that God has raised Him from the dead, you will be saved" (Romans 10:9). Jesus doesn't ask you to simply add Him onto your life. He wants to *be* your life. And to anyone who becomes Jesus's follower, He promises that He will give you a new and pure heart. Second Corinthians 5:17 says, "Old things have passed away; behold, all things have become new."

Believe me when I tell you that without a relationship with Jesus I was a selfish, arrogant, fearful, and materialistic woman. But when I accepted Jesus's free gift of salvation and surrendered my life to Him as my Lord, I was set free. I have never looked back! Jesus took the mess that I was and gave me a new heart. Through Jesus, God forgave all my sins—*all* of them! And when I said yes to entering into a relationship (there's that word again) with Jesus, He put within me His Holy Spirit. (So that's what was missing!) And God wants the same for you.

When God fills you with His Spirit, life makes sense! In fact, it's the life you were born to live, in fellowship with your Creator. Nothing else in this life will ever satisfy your longing for Him—nothing.

If you have a relationship with Jesus, you never have to worry about being "good enough" for God to love you or let you into heaven when you die. To those who are in Christ, God says He adopts us as His very own children: "Behold what manner of love the Father has bestowed on us, that we should be called children of God!" (1 John 3:1). Jesus says we can call God "Abba, Father" (Romans 8:15). That means "daddy." And God says His great love for us is perfect and immeasurable. Nothing we could ever do will make Him stop loving us (Romans 8:35-39)! To top it off, God promises you will never be alone again. Jesus promises He will never leave you nor forsake you (Matthew 28:19-20; Hebrews 13:5).

And there's one more thing: If you decide to believe that Jesus died and rose for you, and you choose to agree with God that you are in need of a Savior because of your sinful heart, and if you pray and submit to Jesus as the Lord of your life, then God's Spirit will fill your heart with His presence, peace, and purpose.

When you receive Jesus's free gift of salvation, He promises to lead you, guide you, and accomplish great things for His kingdom through you for the rest of your life. Ephesians 2:8-10 says, "By grace [that means you can't earn it] you have been saved through faith, and that not of yourselves; it is the gift of God, not of works, lest anyone should boast. For [you] are His workmanship, created in Christ Jesus for good works, which God prepared beforehand." God has a plan for your life.

So now you know what it means to have a relationship with

Jesus. It is my prayer that the Holy Spirit is drawing you to Christ even at this moment, and that you will pray to receive Jesus as your Lord and Savior so you can begin this wonderful journey of walking with Jesus for the rest of your life—then on into heaven in the next!

I would love to celebrate your newfound relationship with Jesus. If you have prayed to receive Christ, won't you let me know?

Rhonda Stoppe
www.rhondastoppe.com/contact

NOTES

Chapter 1—You Are Not Alone

1. Helen Smallbone, *Behind the Lights* (Rocklin, CA: KLove Books, 2022) Introduction.

2. Ken Sande, *The Peacemaker: A Biblical Guide to Resolving Personal Conflict* (Grand Rapids, MI: Baker Books, 2004), 253.

3. Meg Meeker, *Strong Mothers, Strong Sons: Lessons Mothers Need to Raise Extraordinary Men* (New York: Ballantine Books, 2015), xv.

Chapter 2—God Chose You to Be His Mom

1. *The MacArthur Study Bible* (Nashville, TN: Thomas Nelson, 1997), study note for Luke 1:47.

2. *The MacArthur Study Bible,* study note for Luke 1:34.

Chapter 3—Exchanging Your Dreams for God's Plans

1. *The MacArthur Study Bible,* study note for Luke 2:35.

Chapter 5—Train His Brain

1. Paul David Tripp, *Instruments in the Redeemer's Hands: People in Need of Change Helping People in Need of Change* (Phillipsburg, NJ: P&R Publishing, 2002), 260.

2. Tripp, *Instruments in the Redeemer's Hands,* 260.

3. Howard Hendricks, *Teaching to Change Lives: Seven Proven Ways to Make Your Teaching Come Alive* (Colorado Springs: Multnomah, 1987), 17.

Chapter 6—Parenting Without Regrets

1. Tedd and Margy Tripp, *Instructing a Child's Heart* (Wapwallopen, PA: Shepherd Press, 2008), 84.

Chapter 7—Impart the Vision

1. Cindi McMenamin, *Women on the Edge: Turning Desperate Times into Desire for God* (Eugene, OR: Harvest House, 2010), 119.

2. James Stephen, *Twelve Famous Evangelists, with Incidents in Their Remarkable Lives* (London: Pickering & Inglis, n.d.), 8.

3. *The MacArthur Study Bible,* study note for Proverbs 10:9.

4. Emerson Eggerichs, *Mother and Son: The Respect Effect* (Nashville, TN: Thomas Nelson, 2016), 4-5.

5. Hendricks, *Teaching to Change Lives,* 72-73.

Chapter 8—Tools for Autonomy

1. James Dobson, *The New Dare to Discipline* (Wheaton, IL: Tyndale House, 1992), 51.

2. Tripp, *Instruments in the Redeemer's Hands,* 263.

Chapter 9—The Art of Intimacy

1. James Dobson, "Protect Your Kids from Harmful Media," *Dr. James Dobson Family Institute* blog, November 17, 2016, www.drjamesdobson.org/blogs/protect-your-kids-from-harmful-media.

Chapter 10—Conversations That Matter

1. Hendricks, *Teaching to Change Lives*, 72.

2. Tripp, *Instructing a Child's Heart*, 176.

3. Ruth Bell Graham, "Guideposts Classics: Ruth Bell Graham on Faith and Family," *Guideposts*, December 1955, accessed February 17, 2022, www.guideposts.org/inspiration/inspiring-stories/stories-of-faith/guideposts-classics-faith-is-the-ultimate-reward-in.

Chapter 11—The Future That Smiles

1. Arnold Dallimore, *Spurgeon: A New Biography* (Carlisle, PA: The Banner of Truth Trust, 2005), 36.

2. Dallimore, *Spurgeon*, 8-9.

3. Dallimore, *Spurgeon*, 9.

4. Dallimore, *Spurgeon*, 49.

5. D.L. Moody, *Great Joy* (New York: Treat, 1877), 245.

6. Steve Miller, *D.L. Moody on Spiritual Leadership* (Chicago, IL: Moody, 2004), 109.

Chapter 12—You Can Do This

1. John MacArthur, *Twelve Extraordinary Women: How God Shaped Women of the Bible, and What He Wants to Do with You* (Nashville, TN: Thomas Nelson, 2005), 94.

Chapter 13—Even If He Wanders

1. Lawrence Kimbrough, *Words to Die For* (Nashville, TN: Broadman & Holman, 2002), 18.

2. Kimbrough, *Words to Die For*, 18.

3. Kimbrough, *Words to Die For*, 19.

4. Jeanne Hendricks, *A Mother's Legacy* (Colorado Springs, CO: NavPress, 1988), 9.

Chapter 14—Even If You Don't Know What to Say

1. Adapted from Rhonda Stoppe, "When Should I Have the Birds and the Bees Talk with My Kids?" *Crosswalk*, August 15, 2019, www.crosswalk.com/family/parenting/when-should-i-have-the-birds-and-the-bees-talk-with-my-kids.html.

Chapter 15—Even If You're Alone

1. Elyse Fitzpatrick, *Idols of the Heart: Learning to Long for God Alone* (Phillipsburg, NJ: P&R Publishing, 2016), 164.

Chapter 16—Even If You're Scared

1. "Preventing Teen Suicide: Kids in Crisis with Dr. Tim Clinton and Dr. James Dobson," Family Talk Radio, October 20, 2021, https://familytalk.widen.net/view/pdf/rucw8cnbfh/10202021PREVENTINGTEENSUICIDEKIDSINCRISIS.pdf. Used by permission.

2. "Suicide," National Institute of Mental Health, accessed March 3, 2022, https://www.nimh.nih.gov/health/statistics/suicide.

3. Kimbrough, *Words to Die For*, 85.

ACKNOWLEDGMENTS

To my husband, Steve Stoppe—thank you for making our home a place of love and laughter. Thank you for the Christ-honoring example you have been to our children and grand-children. I'm grateful for all your wise counsel and support. You are my favorite!

Thank you, Cindi McMenamin, for taking me by the hand and walking me through the open doors to write this book.

To my editors, Steve Miller and Kathleen Kerr—thank you for patiently working with me to make this book a true and timeless resource. For more than a decade this book has equipped moms who are raising the next generation of godly men. May God establish the work of our hands to use the biblical principles found in this book to guide and estab-lish mothers for generations to come.

ABOUT THE AUTHOR

I could have listened to Rhonda talk all night, is what audiences say about Rhonda Stoppe's messages that weave light-hearted humor and transparent stories together with sound biblical truth. Rhonda is a popular MOPs speaker and best-selling author of seven books. She appears frequently on *Focus on the Family* and *Dobson's Family Talk.* With over 30 years of experience Rhonda helps women:

- discover significance and purpose for their lives
- impact the moral fiber of the next generation by raising children with integrity
- find victory over people-pleasing
- parent without regrets
- enjoy a marriage others dream about
- build an incredible legacy
- become more influential than they ever dreamed possible
- live without regrets

You can connect with Rhonda and get free resources at: www.NoRegretsWoman.com.

Rhonda's family

OLD LADIES KNOW STUFF

with
Rhonda Stoppe
& Friends

LIFE LESSONS

Rhonda's podcast

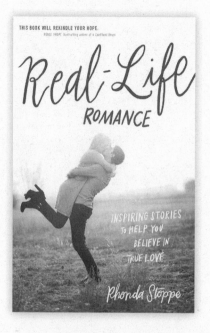

Real-Life Romance

This collection of beautiful, real-life accounts will bring laughter and tears as you enjoy each story of ordinary people who found extraordinary love. Page after page, you will find inspiration to

- rekindle the romance in your love story
- trust in God's providence and timing
- faithfully hope for your own happily-ever-after
- celebrate true romance
- believe in life-long love

Don't let the world define romance for you! See how God is at work in the hearts of His people—knitting together hearts in a love that forever endures.

The Marriage Mentor

Imagine if your good friends were a couple dedicated to help you build the marriage you've always dreamed of.

Steve and Rhonda are that couple. After three decades of helping couples build no-regrets marriages, the Stoppes have compiled their success secrets into this easy-to-read, fun, and interactive book. It will help you ...

- learn to engage in meaningful conversation
- break free from regrets that hold you back
- renew your hope for lifelong love

Every page feels like a candid conversation with a friend. You will laugh and learn from a biblical perspective the secrets to enjoying a marriage that lasts a lifetime.

To learn more about Harvest House books and
to read sample chapters, visit our website:

www.HarvestHousePublishers.com

HARVEST HOUSE PUBLISHERS
EUGENE, OREGON